I0818452

Inside SNC-Lavalin

Inside SNC-Lavalin

How Crime & Politics Almost Killed a Great Canadian Company

Lawrence Stevenson

TORONTO, 2025

Sutherland House
416 Moore Ave., Suite 304
Toronto, ON M4G 1C9

First edition, December 2025

If you are interested in inviting one of our authors to a live event or media appearance, please contact sranasinghe@sutherlandhousebooks.com and visit our website at sutherlandhousebooks.com for more information about our authors and their schedules.

We acknowledge the support of the Government of Canada.

Manufactured in Canada
Cover by Leah Ciani and Jordan Lunn
Book composed by Karl Hunt

Library and Archives Canada Cataloguing in Publication
Title: Inside SNC-Lavalin : how crime and politics almost killed a great Canadian company / Lawrence Stevenson.
Names: Stevenson, Lawrence, author
Description: Includes bibliographical references.
Identifiers: Canadiana (print) 20250225735 | Canadiana (ebook) 20250225743 | ISBN 9781998365531 (softcover) | ISBN 9781997701354 (hardcover) | ISBN 9781998365159 (EPUB)
Subjects: LCSH: SNC-Lavalin—Corrupt practices. | LCSH: Engineering firms—Corrupt practices—Québec (Province) | LCSH: Commercial crimes—Québec (Province) | LCSH: Political corruption—Canada. | LCSH: Corruption investigation—Canada. | LCSH: Fraud investigation—Canada.
Classification: LCC HV6771.C32 Q47 2025 | DDC 364.16/809714—dc23

ISBN (hardcover) 978-1-997701-35-4
ISBN (paperback) 978-1-998365-53-1
eBook 978-1-998365-15-9

Contents

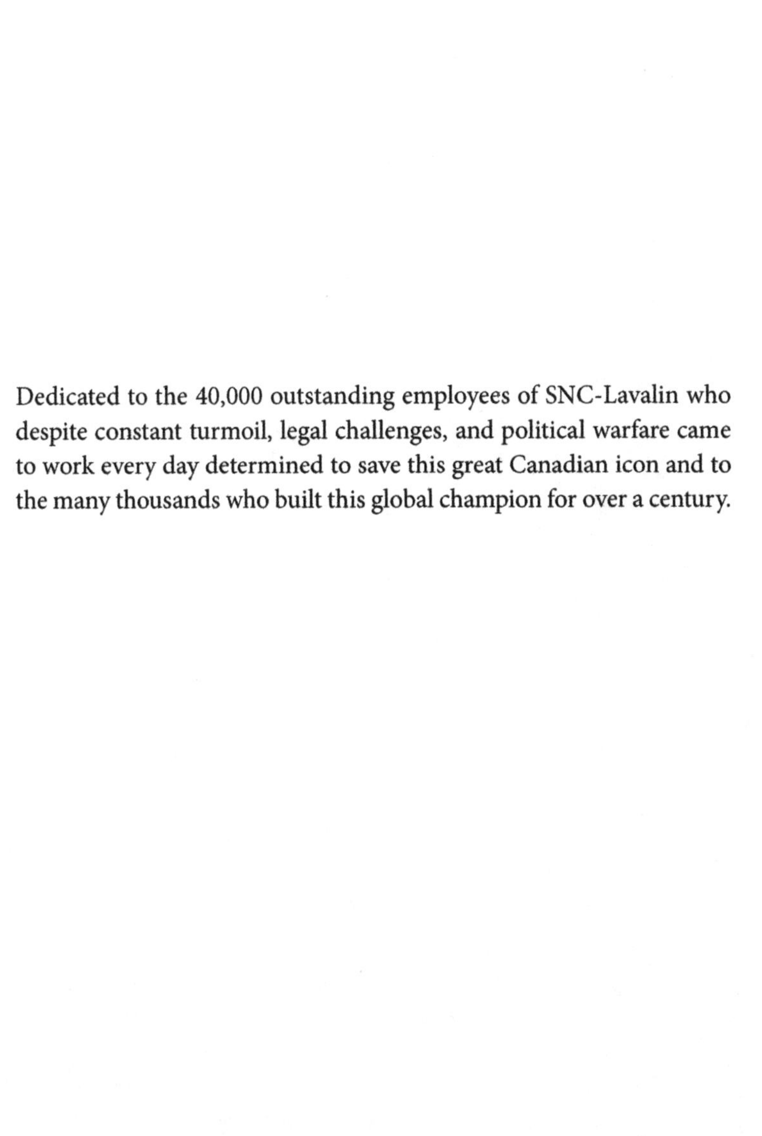

Dedicated to the 40,000 outstanding employees of SNC-Lavalin who despite constant turmoil, legal challenges, and political warfare came to work every day determined to save this great Canadian icon and to the many thousands who built this global champion for over a century.

The only thing necessary for the triumph of
evil is for good men to do nothing.

—attributed to Edmund Burke

Introduction

In early 2019, what became known as the SNC-Lavalin affair threatened to torpedo the Liberal government of Justin Trudeau. Jody Wilson-Raybould, the one-time star justice minister and attorney general, resigned from Cabinet after being shuffled out of her high-profile position. Her fight with Trudeau started over her unwillingness to grant the giant Quebec engineering firm a deferred prosecution agreement (DPA), referred to in Canada as remediation agreement, after it had been charged with bribery.

Trudeau's close friend and top adviser Gerry Butts stepped down shortly after. As did the country's top public servant, Michael Wernick. Both had been pulled into the fight between the prime minister and his justice minister and spat out with bruised reputations.

Another star minister in the Liberal Cabinet, Jane Philpott, followed Wilson-Raybould out the door in protest, citing a loss in confidence in the government's handling of the case. In an interview with a national magazine, she warned that there was more to come.

For months, the country was seized by stories that Trudeau and his office had meddled with the legal system in a coordinated campaign to pressure the attorney general into perverting justice. To anyone reading the headlines throughout this period, it was hard to escape this plot line: a big greedy corporation, in league with some greasy politicians, had tried to steamroll the justice system in search of a get-out-jail-free card over bribery charges. Every major newspaper in the land told this shorthand version of the story.

My version of the SNC-Lavalin affair, is a very different story than what many Canadians who followed the political crisis will recognize.

For eighteen years I sat on the board of SNC-Lavalin. I was with the company through its halcyon days of global growth and dominance. I helped choose three of its CEOs and fought to help guide it through its missteps and crises. In the thick of the company's troubles, I headed the human resources committee and later served as chair of the board. I admit that, as a former insider, I have a bias. But so, too, do those outside observers who often were reporting with only some of the facts. There will be interested parties who will disagree with some of my perspectives based on their own first-hand knowledge of the events that they were a party to. I have tried to get to the truth, but this version of the SNC-Lavalin story is my personal version of what I saw as a director and then chairman of the company. My primary focus is on the period 2011 to 2019 when the SNC-Lavalin affair was front page news.

This book is not the company's perspective nor its rebuttal to the stories that have been written about this affair. This is 100% my own account. I alone am responsible for the point of view articulated on these pages. The company would certainly prefer to forget about this troubled period, but I believe that Canadians need to understand how this tragedy hurt us as a country. This was a monumental own goal. I do not think that justice was served. The individuals who committed the misdeeds got off way too lightly and at the same time a great company spent eight years trying to survive.

A few months ago a business friend of mine was on a flight to Montreal with me. When I told him that I was just finishing a book about the SNC-Lavalin story he was very surprised. He stated that he thought I would want everyone to forget that sorry tale. I told him that I was driven to tell the story as I saw it for three reasons. One is that, contrary to what is written in the press, I think the Board and the management team that took over when the crisis started did an outstanding job to make sure that the company would survive. Which it has. From the minute that the Board was made aware of the nefarious activities they jumped in with both feet to deal with the individuals who had wronged the company and worked to keep this great Canadian company in business. The second reason that I wanted to share my perspectives is because I think this turn of events could happen in any company, to any Board of Directors. A few individuals can work to overcome any set of controls that are put in place. We can all learn from this story.

Finally I think this story underscores a cautionary tale for Canada as we compete in the world market. We cannot put in place laws and regulations that undermine the global competitiveness of our all too few international champions. SNC-Lavalin was hampered by the fact that Canadian laws did not allow for a quick resolution of the issues which would not have been the case in the United States or in the United Kingdom.

This is not a story about a company trying to evade justice or pull political strings. Quite the opposite. From the moment disaster struck—when we were blindsided by the well-hidden crimes of a few top employees—those of us overseeing the company at the board level wrestled with how to get to the bottom of the problem, openly and responsibly, and save a company that was genuinely at risk of total collapse.

The threat of thousands of lost jobs was often seen as a cudgel the company used to threaten the government but SNC-Lavalin was closer than most people realize to going under or being bought and carved up by foreign competitors. It was truly a fight for survival.

The real SNC-Lavalin affair was not really a political thriller at all. Trudeau and Wilson-Raybould's relationship had been breaking down long before SNC-Lavalin's case landed in their laps. The company just had the misfortune to be caught in the crossfire of a Liberal party circular firing squad. That was the political story that captured Canada's headlines for months.

The SNC-Lavalin affair was really a crime story. The crime that started the SNC-Lavalin affair was serious. An executive vice president bribed officials to land lucrative contracts in Libya. The controller of his division was in on the scheme to pay bribes. The company's CEO would also be charged by the authorities. What these senior executives did was wrong. Grievously wrong. Criminally wrong. They *and* the company deserved both blame and punishment. When the issue came to light, these executives were all fired.

SNC-Lavalin deserved punishment for the actions of these senior executives. The company never tried to get off scot-free. Initially this effort was focused on securing a deal with the government that would mean paying a hefty fine, putting in a place a third-party monitor and making sure the individuals responsible were punished. When this failed the company tried to secure a DPA, which in many ways mirrored the deal that the company had tried to arrange with the government.

Let's be perfectly clear: bribery is wrong and should be punished. The problem is that it is systemic even in the western world; one need look no further than the US Supreme Court, where justices accept RVs and luxury vacations. But surely, we should hold ourselves to the same, not a higher, standard than the western countries we compete against.

At the core of the SNC-Lavalin affair is the question of how to punish a corporation for the actions of certain employees without destroying that company or hurting its innocent employees and shareholders—including, in this case, many Quebec pensioners.

At SNC-Lavalin, the board and senior executives would spend years working to reform the company radically. Often lost in the telling of the SNC-Lavalin affair is the fact that we accepted—even welcomed—unprecedented punishment for these crimes.

Yet through much of the affair, we were fighting against a system in which the punishment sought by Canada's top prosecutor was effectively the death penalty—charges that, were the company found guilty, would have banned SNC-Lavalin from bidding on public infrastructure projects, the large engineering firm's very lifeblood. There was virtually no interest in rehabilitation. Prosecutors didn't just drop the ball on this front, they seemed to lack the experience and knowledge about corporate crime to handle the case fairly and efficiently, following precedent set in most other Western nations.

Throughout this period, I watched Canada treat its own companies much more harshly than other western nations do theirs. The US, the UK, Australia, and other Western nations have laws in place to allow for what are known as deferred prosecution agreements, or DPAs. This is a law that, in the case of corporate wrongdoing, defers possible criminal prosecution if the company is willing to put changes and practices in place that will prevent similar crimes in future. They also generally involve sizeable fines and prosecutions of employees who have broken laws. SNC-Lavalin lobbied openly and forcefully for a DPA program in Canada. We didn't want laws that were better, just equal to what existed in other countries that we competed against. Most Canadians would be surprised to learn that many of the companies they do business with, including firms such as Wal-Mart, Airbus, Boeing, Siemens and Rolls-Royce to name a few, have had DPAs. They too did wrong, but their governments did not then try to destroy them.

Canadians are justifiably proud that we play fair. In fact, that is part of our global brand. In 2023 Canada ranked twelfth out of 180 countries in the index compiled by Transparency International, which ranks perceived levels of public sector corruption. The Nordic countries all scored highly while countries such as Yemen, Venezuela, and Somalia ranked at the bottom. In this same index Canada was second only to Germany in the G7. Despite what you may have heard daily in the Canadian press during the SNC-Lavalin affair, Canada is one of the world leaders when it comes to tackling corruption.

The deferred prosecution act that Parliament finally passed in 2018 after much foot dragging was good for Canada. Unfortunately, the then-justice minister was opposed to the law that her own government had just passed. For many Canadians, this rift in the Liberal government marked the beginning of the SNC-Lavalin affair. Before that, it was lost in the business pages.

There is of course blame to go around in this story. The board bears some responsibility for the conduct of its senior officers. Could we have done more to prevent the behaviour of the senior executives who knowingly and surreptitiously broke the law and the company's code of ethics? This is something I've had to reflect on deeply. Along with setting the record straight about what really happened, it's one of the key reasons I want to tell this story.

When I look back at the SNC-Lavalin affair, I'm both saddened and angered by the final tally: Billions of dollars were wasted and lost. A global champion—one of Canada's very, very few—was knocked down. A corporation, which is a legal entity and not a person, cannot be put in prison. SNC-Lavalin was rightly held accountable for the actions of its senior executives. Both the fines and the remediation requirements were fair. Having said that, this file would have been handled very differently in most other western jurisdictions.

Efforts to help an important Canadian company were portrayed as a sinister plot. It was a prime example of a uniquely Canadian anti-business attitude, one that needs to be snuffed out if our small country wants to compete at a global level. I am proudly Canadian and believe that we can go up against the best in the world, but only if our government does not view business as an adversary. As I finish writing this book, we are in the midst of an existential trade war with our most important trading partner. It seems odd to me that Canada would want to put Canadian companies at a disadvantage at this perilous time. We cannot charge our companies carbon taxes if the rest of the world is not doing the same. Just as we should have competitive corporate taxes, capital gains taxes and permitting regulations for pipelines and mines, we should also make sure that the laws of the land create a level playing field. In the SNC-Lavalin case we as a nation tilted the field in favour of our global competitors.

A core group of senior executives betrayed the trust put in them by the many dedicated tens of thousands of employees of the company. The tragedy of the SNC-Lavalin affair is not the political pain that it caused. It's not that certain Cabinet ministers' and political operatives' careers were ended. It is that a company was knocked down and nearly destroyed by its own government. And, at the same time, the three key executives involved did not spend one day in a Canadian jail.

1 | The mystery in Mexico

I first heard the name Cynthia Vanier one day in late 2011.

There was not much on the surface remarkable about Cynthia Vanier. She was from Mount Forest, Ont., a small community northeast of Toronto, where she'd lived for the past eight years with her engineer husband in a modest brick home. They ran a small consulting firm with one other employee out of a Main Street address.

But her life took an abrupt and bizarre turn on November 10 of that year when she was arrested in Mexico and accused by authorities there of being involved in an international plot to smuggle Libyan dictator Muammar Gaddafi's third son, Saadi, into Mexico.

Libya was in the throes of a civil war at the time; Muammar had been assassinated the month before in his hometown of Sirte—dragged from his convoy, beaten, and shot in the side of the head by rebels.

Backed by a coalition of nearly a dozen western nations and supported by NATO bombings—led, coincidentally, by a Canadian, air force lieutenant-general Charles Bouchard—rebel fighters had taken control. Saadi and the rest of the Gaddafi family had fled.

Saadi was the black sheep of the Gaddafi family. Often described as a playboy, he had tried his hand at professional soccer in Italy for a few years—a career fueled by his father's money, not his talent. He briefly hired disgraced sprinter Ben Johnson as his personal trainer. All told, he played as a late substitution in only two games.

He also dabbled in Hollywood, backing a film production company that made a couple of forgettable movies. But he was implicated, too, in the brutality of his father's regime. When it came crashing down, he was a wanted man.

Interpol had recently issued a so-called Red Notice for his arrest, and he was sanctioned for "command of military units involved in repression of demonstrations." A report from the BBC quoted a witness who said Saadi had given orders to fire on unarmed demonstrators. Helping him escape from Libya would put someone very much on the wrong side of the law—and common sense.

Some weeks after Vanier's arrest, Mexico's interior secretary, Alejandro Poire, spelled out the details of the plot to smuggle him into Mexico, saying it was of "international dimensions." He accused Vanier of being "the direct contact with the Gaddafi family and the leader of the group, and presumably was the person in charge of the finances of the operation."

Mexican police had been quietly tracking the group for two months and gathering intelligence. They alleged that Vanier and three co-accused had arranged private flights and prepared forged documents and were negotiating to buy a safe house in Mexico for Gaddafi and his family, who with the help of a bodyguard, allegedly connected to Vanier, had fled to the border with Niger.

"They rented an airplane in order to investigate conditions in the country of Libya and plan the way in which these persons could be extracted and brought to Mexico," read a statement from the Office of the Mexican Attorney General outlining the case. They didn't succeed because the pilots refused to land secretly and remove the family from that nation. Later, they decided to organize a second trip with the safest aircraft for being able to facilitate the extraction and hired a flight company.

Back in Mount Forest, news of her arrest understandably came as a shock. When asked by a local reporter about the bizarre scenario, one resident exclaimed: "Why would somebody like that hide in a little village like Mount Forest?"

Vanier denied the charges. In a letter written from prison, she said she was the "victim of a vicious attack on my professional integrity." Her only connection to Libya, Toronto-based Paul Copeland, her lawyer, said, was that she had been on a fact-finding mission there to prepare a report on the security situation for the Montreal-based engineering and construction giant SNC-Lavalin. Mr. Copeland said she had been in Mexico on business when she was arrested. To imply Vanier was a ringleader in a smuggling operation was absurd, something out of a Tom Clancy novel.

If this all seemed like a wild story to the public, it was no less unbelievable to me and my colleagues on the board of SNC-Lavalin.

Sure, SNC-Lavalin had done business in Libya, just as it had in dozens of other countries. It was one of the world's biggest engineering companies with a hand in everything from mining and oil and gas to infrastructure to nuclear power. But, we were all asking the same question: *Who is Cynthia Vanier?!*

Some quick digging, didn't help ease our confusion. She was a chartered mediator with experience providing dispute resolution services primarily on behalf of First Nations communities. Why in the world would the company have hired *her* to do work as a consultant in Libya?

The situation got stranger still when we found that Stéphane Roy had also been detained in Mexico on charges related to those against Vanier. Stéphane Roy was a name we knew well. He was an SNC-Lavalin vice-president and controller in our construction division—the company's biggest and most important.

Roy was riding in the back of a large black SUV on November 11, after checking in to the Mexico City Four Seasons Hotel, when his vehicle was surrounded by police officers. With him were two people that police said were connected to the alleged Vanier plot. At a police station in Mexico City, he explained he was a vice-president at a large Canadian company and that he was in the country for work on a water treatment project. He was released and headed straight home for Montreal.

Vanier was not so lucky. She remained inside Mexico's prison system, in jail near the Belize border, in what were no doubt appalling conditions.

Back at SNC-Lavalin, we had way more questions than answers: what was Roy doing in Mexico of all places, a country where SNC-Lavalin did very little business? He was well liked within the company and had a reputation as a hell of a nice guy, eager to go along to get along and not cause ripples.

How had someone like this and a small-town mediator become accused of a plot pulled from the pages of an action-thriller—and now making headlines around the world?

The only common thread here was that SNC-Lavalin had once had dealings with the Gaddafi family, including Saadi, through its work in the country dating back over a decade. All contracts to do business in Libya ran through the Gaddafi family, and any number of big multinational firms who worked in Libya—as well as most Western leaders including prime ministers of Canada and the UK—had shaken hands with the Gaddafis. But when the civil war broke out, our operations had ground to a halt and our employees evacuated for safety reasons.

If someone connected to the company was plotting a smuggling operation, they were operating way outside the lines.

At the same time that we were scratching our heads about Cynthia Vanier and Stéphane Roy, another unwelcome surprise landed in our laps in the form of an anonymous letter, personally addressed to most members of the SNC-Lavalin board as well as CEO Pierre Duhaime, CFO Gilles Laramee and a few major shareholders. And unlike the inexplicable case in Mexico, this struck us right away as a potential bombshell.

Like other companies of similar size and sophistication, SNC-Lavalin had an HR-managed whistle-blower program encouraging employees to report serious breaches in policy or ethics without risking their position within the firm. Anonymous letters weren't unusual. But letters forwarded to the personal attention of board members, shareholders plus the CEO and CFO sure were.

The letter that landed in our inboxes was poorly written and full of spelling mistakes, but it grabbed our attention. The writer claimed that Riadh Ben Aissa, the company's executive vice-president of the infrastructure division, was a shady character who was not to be trusted.

Among other things, the letter writer said Ben Aissa had been making sweetheart deals benefitting himself and his family. They claimed, for instance, that his family actually owned the building SNC-Lavalin leased as its headquarters in Tunisia. Rent money may have been going straight into his and his family's pocket.

Ben Aissa, a Tunisian-born Canadian, was the most important division head at the company, responsible for many of SNC-Lavalin's biggest deals and projects in recent times. He had a well-earned reputation as a "firefighter," the term used inside the company for someone who could turn around troubled projects. Was there a problem in Ankara? A big opportunity in Saudi Arabia? Send Ben Aissa, the thinking went.

When hell broke loose in Libya in 2010, it was Ben Aissa who stepped up when there were no flights or ships available to evacuate our employees. He found a fleet of buses and got the job done, earning a round of applause from those of us on the board.

Under the previous CEO, Jacques Lamarre, Ben Aissa had also earned an enormous degree of freedom in how he ran his division—and he did it well. He had almost single-handedly built SNC-Lavalin's business in the Middle East.

Despite the fact that the letter's sender was unidentified, and the charges lacked any hard evidence, it could not be ignored. But we had to tread carefully. For all we knew, the letter might have been penned by some disgruntled employee making wild claims to destroy a high-flying senior exec's reputation. We decided that the best way to respond was to direct the human resources team to look into the allegations.

At our board meeting in early December, one of half a dozen we'd have each year on the twenty-first floor of SNC-Lavalin's glass-faced headquarters in Montreal, this worrying letter and the mystifying Vanier-Roy question were raised, albeit briefly. We had no reason to think these two events were in any way connected or more than strange anomalies.

Our message to the CEO was, "Let's get to the bottom of this." Duhaime promised he would find out more and report back.

As the board meeting wrapped up, we marked the end of another successful calendar year. SNC-Lavalin had projects going in 100 countries, it had 28,000 employees, a net income of $379 million, and cash reserves of over $1 billion. The stock price had hit an all-time high that year, $60 per share. And SNC-Lavalin had just celebrated its hundredth anniversary with a splashy gala reception in Montreal, attended by over 1,000 guests including the who's who of corporate Canada. Many ambassadors and senior political figures were present, and Quebec premier Jean Charest gave a speech congratulating the company on its tremendous success.

In celebration of that milestone, the company had even published a coffee table book, *SNC-Lavalin: The First 100 Years*. Wrote CEO

Duhaime in the preface: "At a moment in time such as this, it is impossible not to speculate about what the next 100 years hold for SNC Lavalin. The world will continue to evolve in ways no one can foresee."

Those words today are almost laughable. Indeed, the company would evolve in ways no one could have foreseen. Like a CEO appearing on the cover of *Fortune*, or a hockey team prematurely celebrating a shut-out, Duhaime seemed to be tempting fate.

By the time the board would meet again for its next regularly scheduled meeting in March, things would look radically different. Those strange events back in November 2011 would prove to be hairline cracks in the foundation of one of Canada's most successful, important companies. And they were about to split open catastrophically, harming thousands of employees and shareholders, erasing the SNC-Lavalin name, and very nearly destroying the company.

And on a personal level, it was about to upend my life and work in a way I could never have predicted when I became a part of the SNC-Lavalin story.

2 | The buck stops where?

Growing up in northern Quebec, in the mining town of Chibougamau, my one dream was to fly planes. My dad, named James but known to all as Scotty because of his thick accent, had been a bush pilot and taught me to fly at a young age. Skipping school to go flying with him was a joy that far outweighed the heavy-handed punishment I faced from my Catholic school teachers when I landed.

Scotty came to Canada from Scotland at the age of sixteen. He flew high-speed, twin-engined Mosquito fighter-bombers during the war, first as a flying instructor from 1939 to 1941 at the base in St. Hubert, then overseas from 1941 to 1945. He'd flown with a number of Royal Military College (RMC) grads, and he thought the world of them. When it came time for me to go to university, the choice was obvious: RMC. I didn't apply anywhere else.

RMC proved a perfect fit. I did well, finishing top of my class in basic officer training and then graduating as the top cadet. But a routine medical showed that I needed glasses. That was the end of my dreams of being a jet fighter pilot.

I studied economics and commerce, and after graduation joined the Princess Patricia's Canadian Light Infantry and then the Canadian Airborne Regiment as a platoon commander. I served two peacekeeping tours in Cyprus.

But I had decided that my future lay in business, not soldiering, and in 1982 I was accepted to do an MBA at Harvard.

For Harvard students at the time, the hottest ticket in town was the management consulting firm Bain and Company. Each fall companies came to present to students at Burden Hall. Some big names showed up, like GE's legendary CEO Jack Welch, but no one filled the room like Bain's Mitt Romney. Like many of the people in the room that day, after listening to him I knew where I wanted to work.

As luck would have it, I got a summer job with the firm working in London. A full-time job offer followed. By November of the next year, I was working forty hours a week for Bain commuting to a client in New Jersey, while also (foolishly, I now realize) working through my final year at Harvard and waking up at 5 a.m. to get my pilot's license, all while trying to pay down my student debt. It was exhausting, but somehow, I made it through.

I spent five years in the Bain London office and was promoted to partner in under four years. By 1989, I was heading up Bain and Company Canada, with Romney becoming my boss after a management shakeup. It was at Bain where I first took an interest in SNC-Lavalin. The company was created in 1991 with the merger of Lavalin, a conglomerate with interests in everything from real estate to oil refining to aircraft leasing, and SNC, one of Canada's premier engineering and construction companies. The merger, spurred by Lavalin's brush with bankruptcy, created a Quebec powerhouse—a new company with extensive international experience.

Shortly after the merger, I was introduced to CEO Guy Saint-Pierre by my personal friend and mentor, Jean Ostiguy, who ran one of Canada's largest and most successful investment banks. I wanted to convince Guy that Bain could help him develop a strategy for the newly merged company. We had done significant work in both mergers and acquisitions and specific work in the engineering and construction sector. It was a good fit, and Guy was open to hearing more.

Guy Saint-Pierre was one of the most impressive CEOs I worked with during my years at Bain and Company. He had served as Quebec's minister of industry and commerce and then left politics to become a senior vice president at Labatt Breweries. He, like me, had a military background having served in the Royal Canadian Engineers (I had also spent a summer learning demolitions as an engineer in Chilliwack, BC). We both often reminisced about our times in the training fields of Gagetown, N.B., where I spent four summers during my time in the Canadian Army. He was a true officer and a gentleman. His diplomatic skills were needed to merge the two different cultures of SNC and Lavalin.

I was keen to work for Canadian companies that I believed could be global champions, and my team and I threw ourselves into the work. We prepared an extensive study to develop a strategy for SNC-Lavalin. And after seven months of work with the company's senior executives, it was ready to be presented.

In April 1992, in a hotel conference room out on Montreal's West Island, I spent two hours outlining the plan to the board of directors, an impressive collection of high-profile Canadian businesspeople and former politicians including legendary investor Stephen Jarislowsky and former Quebec premier Pierre-Marc Johnson.

At its core, the strategy was to take the company's strength in engineering and construction that it had built in Quebec and use it to compete internationally in such sectors as hydro power, mining, aluminum smelting, among others, where, when it came to competing for projects, SNC-Lavalin were already in the top five companies in that sector.

Bain & Company has studied more than 4,000 companies and found that, in any industry, eighty percent of the profit pie goes to the number one or two player in that industry.

The Bain team divided the company's revenue into three buckets: market leaders; players (not the market leader but a strong position); and followers (a very weak market position). A fuller discussion on the value of market share can be found in the Appendix at the end of this book. As the chart overleaf shows the leaders and players, as defined by their relative market share (RMS) generated sixty percent of SNC-Lavalin's sales but more than 100 percent of its profits. Business in this category included aluminum smelters, nuclear and hydro. Our advice was to invest more in these businesses and to seriously evaluate the 40 percent of the company that generated no profits.

This forty percent included businesses, like oil and gas, where SNC-Lavalin was a very small global competitor. Bain's advice was to either go big in a few of these areas through acquisition or else exit these businesses—they were a distraction. Often in strategy it is more important to highlight what you will not do. What business sectors or segments you will not go after.

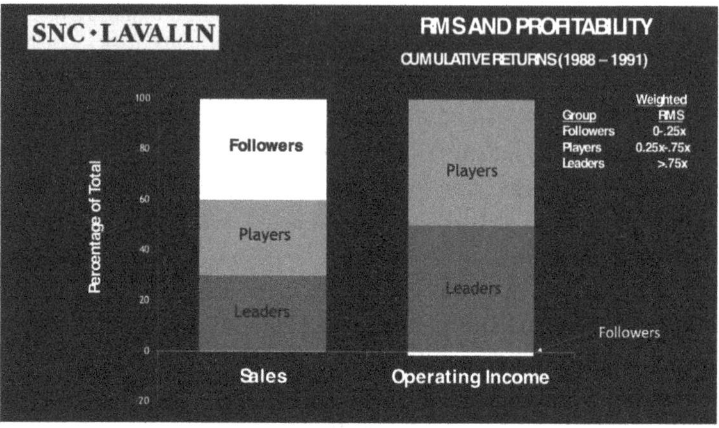

The SNC Lavalin plan was a success. The company agreed that its security division, Securiplex, should be sold, and a few years later the Canadian munitions division, Canadian Arsenals, was also sold. Under Guy Saint-Pierre's leadership, SNC-Lavalin thrived. In 1993 he was chosen as CEO of the year by the *Financial Post.*

Two years later, Saint-Pierre decided it would soon be time for him to hang up his skates; his chosen successor was Jacques Lamarre. It's here, in the Lamarre era, that SNC-Lavalin really started to shoot up the ranks of global engineering powerhouses. It seemed it could do no wrong as Jacques expanded the company's footprint enormously and the company's earnings and stock price soared higher and higher.

It's also possible to trace some of SNC-Lavalin's key faults back to this phase. These were like minor miscalculations made in its early construction. They were not visible at the time, but they would pull the whole organization off kilter as it grew bigger and bigger.

* * *

Jacques Lamarre came from the Lavalin side of the SNC-Lavalin merger. Born in Jonquiere in northern Quebec, very close to where I grew up, he was a graduate of Laval University and joined the company in 1967. The person you would put on any difficult project, he had learned project management from the ground up at Lavalin, under the coaching of his brother, and then-CEO, Bernard Lamarre.

Jacques had delivered projects on time and on budget in virtually every corner of the globe. He had successfully led projects in Benin and in Niger and had recently completed the very successful Ankara metro project. Under his leadership, the transportation division grew from virtually nothing to become the company's main profit generator. In some respects, he was the Ben Aissa of his time—the company's original firefighter and rainmaker.

He had learned the skills in the school of hard knocks, not in Ivy League classrooms. He would surely have hated the idea of an outside consultant like me coming in to tell him what's best for the company. (Although, he would eventually end up taking a three-month executive management course at Harvard.)

Lamarre officially became CEO at the annual general meeting in 1996. *Commerce* magazine put him on the cover with the headline "Jacques the Conqueror." By the mid-2000s, he had created what many would call a "planetary powerhouse."

I joined the board of SNC-Lavalin shortly after, in 1999, invited on the basis of my work with Bain & Company, and my own experience as a CEO. And I had a front-row seat through this period of rapid growth. Jacques built an amazing global enterprise and would in 2002, like Saint-Pierre, be chosen as Canada's CEO of the year. SNC-Lavalin was one of the few Canadian companies to ever have two different CEOs recognized as CEO of the year.

Jacques was one of the best CEOs I'd ever seen. His wife once told me that he chose their vacation destinations by considering where SNC-Lavalin was doing major projects in the world. He would always drop in to visit with the project leaders and the employees working there. He lived and breathed SNC-Lavalin.

Jacques' primary objective was building a great company. He was driven by that and not money or fame. In fact, he avoided the limelight. He was one of the few CEOs that I have known in my time in business who was not a strong negotiator with respect to his own compensation. In my ten years as chair of the human resource committee, he never complained or tried to push for a bigger salary, larger bonus or more long-term incentives for himself.

But there was a very important distinction to be made about Jacques Lamarre. He was obsessed with the company, but he was not a micromanager by any stretch. Jacques knew all the details but the SNC-Lavalin he built featured a highly decentralized and entrepreneurial culture. He expected the business leaders to drive their own businesses. Individual executives were the hunters and were expected to generate business without a lot of input from a central office. There was an unspoken directive: Do what it takes to win the business.

Lavalin, before the merger, had a strong "Eat what you kill and get the job done" corporate culture. How well you did was entirely related to the business you brought in. Even though it was SNC that took over Lavalin, it was this culture that prevailed under Lamarre.

Culture, in my opinion, is the DNA of an organization. Years ago, when I had acquired both SmithBooks and Coles to form Chapters, I was amazed to find that the culture of the two organizations still lived on in the individuals who had worked at either firm, years after we had merged. Culture is the most difficult thing to change in an organization.

All great companies have a strong culture and SNC-Lavalin under Jacques Lamarre was no exception. Companies with strong cultures tend to promote from within. When I was the CEO of Pep Boys from 2003 to 2006, I wanted to hire people from our strongest competitor, Discount Tire. But people would not leave Discount Tire, as everyone had started at the bottom and worked their way up the ladder. Discount Tire employees lived the company culture every day and could never imagine working anywhere else. The same is true at Costco which is arguably the greatest retailer of this generation. Jacques built this winning culture at SNC-Lavalin. Under Jacques every single promotion to the office of the president was from within the company. This winning culture helped propel the company's superior performance.

If Lamarre could have got away with it, he would not have had anyone in the head office. As a public company, he acknowledged at least that he needed a CFO. But he didn't like the costs. Why, for example, do we need an HR department, he once asked me, to my surprise. In many ways he was following the playbook of many very successful CEOs, such as Percy Barnevik at ABB, the multinational electrical engineering firm. Barnevik was a strong believer in radical decentralization, and he set up more than 5,000 profit centers at ABB. It clearly worked as the company under his leadership increased its stock value by a factor of eighty-seven.

Jacques' view was that you need five or six people who run different parts of the world, and you let them be the CEO of that region and don't get in their hair. "Let them do the role that I was allowed to do when I was in that position," he argued. His view of the board was similarly hands-off. Let me do my job or throw me out.

As one director commented to me, "Jacques would have preferred to not have to report to a board. He viewed SNC-Lavalin as his business." Jacques made many acquisitions during his tenure, but these were always "tuck-ins" rather than large bet-the-company moves. He was a calculated risk-taker as he would prove with his stunning successful investment in Highway 407 in Ontario. Like all good poker players, he understood that the trick was to "know when to hold 'em, know when to fold 'em." He fought when he was right but he also backed down when he viewed the fight as unwinnable, as when we lost serious money on a large power project, for example.

The lack of centralization that he favored didn't bother me. It played to his strengths. Lamarre was an expert in the business, one who commanded respect. Everyone who worked for him was intimidated by him to some extent, which kept things in check. And it was hard to argue with the results: year after year, the company under his watch posted big wins. This was not an Enron; these were real numbers and a great business.

When he left in 2009, after forty-two years at the company, Lamarre passed on a wildly successful firm. During his thirteen years at the helm, Jacques had increased revenues dramatically and had quadrupled the number of employees working for SNC-Lavalin. He had taken the market capitalization of the company from $400 million to $6 billion. Like Guy Saint-Pierre before him, Jacques would be honoured by being inducted into the Canada Business Hall of Fame.

Unlike Lamarre, who grew as a CEO along with the company, Pierre Duhaime would have to start at a full-out sprint. For any CEO, it would be a huge challenge to keep the music going—and a tremendous one for a new CEO.

Harder still, Pierre inherited this incredibly decentralized organization, with fiefdoms both loyal to Lamarre and free to operate as they saw fit. Nobody feared Pierre Duhaime. He had inherited a finely tuned machine, and he was keen to not break it. Pierre was also inheriting, as we would find out in a few years, some very questionable practices in the Middle East, led by Riadh Ben Aissa and his predecessor Sami Bebawi.

Pierre didn't just have to fill some very big shoes; he was walking into a minefield.

In the weeks after our December board meeting, more details about Cynthia Vanier, Riadh Ben Aissa, and Stéphane Roy were being uncovered, sparking a flurry of activity—and anxiety—inside the company.

For starters, it was true that Roy had contracted Vanier to launch a fact-finding mission in Libya when the war broke out. The stated aim was to assess the situation and what it meant for the company and its operations there.

Vanier traveled into the country, by then a war zone, via private jet and produced a five-page report, sympathetic to the Gaddafi regime. The company paid her more than $100,000. The report was an embarrassment, and the fact that it had even been produced by someone with no expertise or experience was worrying.

We quickly uncovered there was much more going on than this backwards report. The smuggling plot was real, and it was tied to SNC-Lavalin.

Roy had connected with Vanier through Gary Peters, the head of a Canadian private security company. In 2008, Peters had been hired by SNC-Lavalin to provide security for Saadi on his trip to Canada. He had joined Vanier on her trip to Libya.

We would later find out that Roy had advanced $650,000 from SNC-Lavalin's construction division to Vanier and Peters, who assembled a team of ex-military personnel. A few months later they all met, along with Ben Aissa, at the Queen Elizabeth Hotel in Montreal, according to Vincent Larouche's deeply reported book on the subject, *La Saga SNC-Lavalin.*

One ex-soldier told Larouche the mission was a clown show. "I had concerns right from the start," he said. "Peters had this big SAS tattoo on his arm. I was in the SAS for ten years and we had no tattoos like that. Never. He told me it was in honour of a friend who had died. Peters believed his own lies. He said he had made 3,000 free fall parachute jumps. I don't know anyone who has done that." I served in the

Canadian Airborne Regiment, and I never met anyone who had done 3,000 jumps.

In interviews with the press, Peters would later say Vanier had been brought on only to get travel and identity documents for Saadi, but that they were to be obtained legally. How, I wondered, might one "legally" get travel documents for a person wanted for potential war crimes?

On December 30, 2011, I joined a call with other board members to discuss the Mexico caper. The details were disturbing enough that the board elected to hire our own outside legal counsel.

Duhaime, meanwhile, was downplaying the situation. On January 9, 2012, he had dinner in Calgary with Ian Bourne, who headed the board's audit committee. When Riadh Ben Aissa's name came up Duhaime said, "There's nothing to worry about."

A few days later, company lawyers interviewed Roy and he finally acknowledged what was going on. All in, SNC-Lavalin appeared to have paid Vanier $1.8 million—money that was used to hire the mercenaries and private jets and cover other costs involved in trying to get Saadi out of North Africa.

The company was pulling on a thread that was unraveling trouble upon trouble. On top of this stunning smuggling plot, SNC-Lavalin money had been spent to cover the fees for Saadi's Toronto condo. He had bought it while on a three-month-long trip to Canada in 2008 hosted by SNC-Lavalin. These payments were more than unacceptable, they were illegal. In March 2011, the UN had ordered Gaddafi family assets frozen.

But the most alarming discovery, made by a SNC-Lavalin finance controller, was that company funds from Ben Aissa's division appeared to be going into accounts that could not be identified. Ben Aissa's division seemed to be a tangle of secrets and questionable conduct.

By this time, Ben Aissa was feeling the heat. He told his Swiss bankers and lawyers to "prepare a fortress against the demands that will come from Canada," according to Larouche's reporting. On top of the questions being asked and investigators probing his division, the uprisings of the Arab Spring in 2010 and 2011 threatened to undo all his work and dismember his prized network of contacts.

The troubles left Pierre Duhaime deeply rattled too, despite what he'd told Bourne. These were the kind of revelations that cost CEOs their jobs.

Board Chair Gwyn Morgan was in Hong Kong for an HSBC board meeting when he got a call outlining the unauthorized payments. "The following 16 months turned out to be the most disturbing and challenging of my four-decade career in business," he would later write in an op-ed in the *Globe and Mail.*

On February 9, the board decided to part ways with both Ben Aissa and Roy. As for the missing funds, we retained our external auditor Deloitte & Touche to look at the unauthorized payments and where they might have gone.

We could hardly believe what was happening to a company that just a few months before was on top of the world. It seemed "surreal," Morgan wrote. "SNC-Lavalin had recently celebrated 100 years of progress to becoming one of the world's most respected engineering and construction firms. I hoped that it was all some sort of accounting mix-up."

Normally the board met every three months. Throughout February, we gathered weekly.

The unauthorized transfers appeared to have gone into two accounts, and were meant to pay commercial agents hired to help win two big infrastructure contracts through our office in Tunisia. We still did not know who was behind those accounts. We had to face facts: we would not be able to report financial results on time.

The morning of the meeting was a dark and ominously cloudy day. Inside the boardroom at SNC-Lavalin, we were all in an equally foul mood.

We came to the realization that we had no choice but to report the missing funds to the authorities. We would have to put out a press release disclosing that we would not be able to release our financial results and that the company would miss its net income target by a whopping eighteen percent, or about $80 million.

The stock was about to get hammered.

Indeed, the share price, which had slipped following news reports of the employee detained in Mexico, went into free fall, dropping twenty-one percent in value overnight. The moment the news came out, I fielded half a dozen calls from friends who worked on Wall Street and Bay Street demanding to know what was going on.

Answers would take time, but I knew what action needed to be taken next. This was Pierre Duhaime's responsibility, and he would have to go.

We had an ideal candidate to replace Pierre Duhaime. Ian Bourne, a strong board director who spent much of his business career at GE and was known for his high level of integrity, was ready and willing to do it. No one was more qualified to help guide the company through what would surely be the most difficult period to this point in its 100-year history.

The day Stéphane Roy was let go; he handed a yellow folder to CFO Gilles Laramee on his way out the door. Inside were details about two shell companies, called Dinova and Duvel that the SNC-Lavalin funds had been funneled into. It also mentioned another payout to a third mysterious company called Sierra Management. This one had nothing to do with the Middle East. It appeared to be connected to a project in the company's own backyard, Montreal.

There was something seriously wrong happening inside SNC-Lavalin.

3 | Eat what you kill

At 6:25 p.m. on December 21, 1988 a Boeing 747 lifted off from London's Heathrow heading for New York's John F. Kennedy International Airport. Named *Clipper Maid of the Seas*, the plane was one of the original jumbo jets.

Thirty minutes into the flight the 747 was cruising at 31,000 ft. At exactly 7:03 p.m., the cockpit voice recorder captured a loud noise. Air traffic control radar showed five objects where there should have been one. Pan Am Flight 103 had been blown apart by a virtually undetectable explosive called Semtex that had been placed inside a hard-shell Samsonite suitcase.

That suitcase was loaded onto the aircraft in Malta by Libyan intelligence agents. The bomb killed 243 passengers and 16 crew. Pieces of the aircraft, engulfed in flames, also killed 11 residents in the town of Lockerbie, Scotland. One section of the plane, full of jet fuel, landed on a neighborhood and exploded, leaving a forty-foot deep crater.

I had been on Pan Am 103 the previous night.

A few years ago, I visited Lockerbie. I spent a memorable half day with a Lockerbie resident, Colin Dorrance. Back in 1988, Colin had just recently graduated from his constable training. As a young eighteen-year-old he was back home in Lockerbie to spend the Christmas holidays with his parents. In the early evening on December 21, Colin was driving to a holiday party when he was confronted by an enormous fireball two hundred yards in front of his car. He thought it was a vehicle explosion. It turned out to have been a part of Pan Am 103.

Colin would spend the next several days with many other constables gathering bodies and protecting the very large crime scene. As part of his duties, Colin would bring some of the bodies into the temporary morgue set up in the gymnasium in Lockerbie's town hall. One of the victims Colin had to carry into that morgue was the youngest victim on Pan Am 103, a two-month-old baby named Bryony Owen. She had been traveling from Wales to Boston with her mother Yvonne to visit family in the United States for the Christmas holidays. A farmer brought her body to town after having found her in a field at the back of his farm. "It was a young child," Colin recounted. "It looked as though they were asleep, it wasn't obviously injured, and it was a shock to realize it was a passenger from Pan Am 103."

Thirty-five of the passengers were young Syracuse University students studying in the UK for a semester who were heading home for Christmas. As we drove around town, Colin told me about two of them. Nicole Boulanger had recently celebrated her twenty-first birthday on October 28, 1988. As we passed a small house in Lockerbie, Colin pointed out the home of a woman named Josephine Donaldson. It was on Carlisle Road, only two hundred yards away from Sherwood Crescent where five houses were completely destroyed when they were hit by the wing section of Pan Am 103.

Josephine woke up the next morning to find a perfectly placed purse in her garden. When she opened the purse, she noticed several birthday cards for Nicole. Later Josephine would see video of a woman on TV screaming, distraught, on the floor at JFK airport as she learned that her daughter was not coming home. This was Nicole's mom, Jeanine.

Many months later when the police had finished their forensic investigation and prepared to release personal items back to families, Josephine and several other Lockerbie residents volunteered to clean and iron the 22,000 items of clothing and property that had fallen from the sky. Josephine was cleaning an art portfolio bag when she was astonished to discover twenty-first birthday cards in this bag. The bag also belonged to a Syracuse University student, Amy Beth Shapiro. She, too, had turned twenty-one on October 28, 1988.

Twice a year Josephine lays flowers in the Lockerbie Garden of Remembrance for "her two girls"—once on the anniversary of Pan Am 103 in December and again on October 28. In 2018 Colin arranged for Josephine to travel to Syracuse to mark the thirtieth anniversary. Josephine met Nicole's mom Jeanine for the first time.

Colin escorted me to a vast field just outside Lockerbie where the most iconic photo of Pan Am 103 was taken, the one showing the front section of the fuselage with most of the plane's name, clearly visible. This field had particular significance for me personally as three of the passengers who were on that fateful flight were my friends: Nicholas Bright, Peter Dix, and Andre Guevorgian.

Nicholas and Andre had been classmates of mine at Harvard, and both Nicholas and Peter were colleagues of mine at Bain & Company. I admired them immensely. Nicholas and Peter had just started families, as had I. All three had been sitting in the business class section of Pan Am 103 and they came to rest in this wide-open field. These admirable young men were at the very start of brilliant lives. Peter was an Olympic athlete and had been booked on the British Airways flight that night, but tragically he switched to Pan Am when he ran into Nicholas at the airport.

Nicholas and I had worked closely together over the previous six months. I'd been promoted to partner the summer before, and Nicholas was a manager in the Boston office, heading up one of my teams. He was a superstar. One of the last conversations I had with Nicholas was several weeks before, when we were both about to board a flight at Gatwick airport. Nicholas instructed me to never stand in the open concourse of an airport. When I asked him why he told me that the people who survive bombings are always those standing near structural columns. It was a curious factoid, and one I can't shake when I think of Nicholas on Pan Am 103.

After he and Peter Dix were killed, Bain & Company started giving an annual award called The Bright-Dix prize to the consultant who gave back most to the community. The world had lost three amazing individuals but every one of the 243 passengers on Pan Am 103 was a son, daughter, brother, sister, mother, or father. So many families would never be the same.

Those behind the bombing had committed an especially vile terrorist act, pure and simple. Soon after the bombing, it became clear that the act had not only been carried out by two identified Libyans but was undoubtedly sanctioned by Gaddafi. It wasn't until 1999 that they were finally handed over to the UN to stand trial. And in 2003 Gaddafi finally accepted Libya's responsibility for the bombing, hoping in exchange that economic sanctions on his country would be lifted.

I don't hold grudges. But I do retain memories, and my memory of my friends, these three bright hard-working guys who perished aboard Flight 103, with young families waiting for them at home, coloured my assessment of Gaddafi and put me off ever being associated with him. When SNC-Lavalin hosted Saadi Gaddafi at a reception in Montreal in 2008, I politely sent an email to Jacques Lamarre declining my invitation. I told Jacques I understood why we do business in Libya and that I was not trying to take a stand, I just would not shake hands or be in the same room as Muammar Gaddafi's son.

The number one question I get from serious businesspeople, when we get into talking about the SNC-Lavalin affair, is *Why were you guys in Libya in the first place?* There is a sense that SNC-Lavalin got what it deserved playing in that part of the world. As one person put it to me, "You guys were playing with fire when you played with Gaddafi, and you got burned."

A part of me agrees with this. Libya came to represent a substantial chunk of SNC-Lavalin's business. Its vast oil holdings represented a potential to earn massive profits from the country's planned infrastructure projects. But doing business there inevitably meant dealing with Gaddafi, a man widely remembered as "the mad dog of the Middle East," responsible not just for an act of heinous terrorism over Scotland but for terrorizing his own people.

That was certainly a version of Gaddafi—call it Version 1.0. But there was another version, and it explains why SNC-Lavalin ended up so invested in Libya.

Version 2.0 of Gaddafi was created in a ceremonial Bedouin tent on the outskirts of Tripoli, on a Thursday in March 2004. In what became known as "The Deal in the Desert," a handshake from British Prime Minister Tony Blair brought Gaddafi in from the cold, marking his transformation from terrorist bankroller and tyrant to darling of the business world.

Gaddafi had agreed to dismantle Libya's weapons of mass destruction—probably having learned a valuable lesson from what happened to Saddam Hussein—and throw open the doors for Western business leaders to Libya's vast resources.

Blair's office quickly announced that Royal Dutch/Shell had signed a $200-million deal to drill for oil and natural gas off the Libyan coast.

More leaders would beat a path to Gaddafi's tent: French President Jacques Chirac, German Chancellor Gerhard Schroeder, Italian Premier Silvio Berlusconi.

Libya's opening, said Blair after the meeting, "gives us real hope that we can build a new relationship with it, one for the modern world. . . . Times change. And when they do change, we should be prepared to change with them, provided the changes are real."

By the end of 2004, it was Canadian Prime Minister Paul Martin's turn to shake Gaddafi's hand. Martin's trip was widely regarded at home as a positive step. And SNC-Lavalin, the expert in building the infrastructure Libya needed, was at the top of the list of companies ready to take advantage of the new, warm relations.

Lamarre had been a big proponent of Martin's trip—one of the company's early mega-projects was the $230-million Great Man-Made River project in Libya, bringing water across the Sahara Desert to cities in the north of the country. By 2004 SNC-Lavalin was on the cusp of landing a new $1-billion deal there. It would even go on to build a prison in the country, a project that would later become controversial.

Lamarre saw SNC-Lavalin's expansion into places like Libya, Algeria, and Saudi Arabia as a kind of modern-day manifest destiny. "We like win-win situations," he said in an interview with the *Globe and Mail* in 2006. "We've been involved in international markets for over forty years and have helped many countries to become normal. With us, they see the Canadian way—the freedom we have, the relationship we have with our government." Years before his brother Bernard Lamarre, then the CEO at Lavalin, had said similar sentiments to *La Presse*: "We have the competence of the Americans, without their foreign policy."

In a lot of the countries where SNC-Lavalin set up, relations with governments and government officials were very different than the "Canadian way." Most ranked high on Transparency International's Bribe Payers Index. You had to be concerned about corruption in parts of the world where it was an accepted part of doing business.

I was supportive of SNC-Lavalin's strategy to enter these markets. In the Bain and Co. plan I'd presented to SNC-Lavalin, we advised that the company should focus on parts of the world that met three criteria.

First, they should be medium-sized countries, since it would be hard to displace local incumbents in large markets. Second, we should avoid markets where the Americans, who were represented by some of the largest worldwide firms (such as Bechtel), were dominant. American geopolitical wizardry would be too much for Canadian-based SNC-Lavalin. Promises of American aid and contracts for vital defence requirements, such as F15 fighter aircraft, would always win against any package that Canada could offer. This meant looking for international opportunities in markets where the Americans were less welcome including, at the time, many parts of Asia, such as Vietnam.

The third criteria was to focus on countries where SNC-Lavalin had already done well and built a strong franchise and where there was a natural cultural affinity. We recommended focusing more on countries such as Algeria and Tunisia where SNC Lavalin could become a major player. This would also help the company to concentrate on those countries that needed the engineering experience they had built in Canada.

As separate companies SNC and Lavalin had both done quite well internationally before the merger. Partly this was because as relatively small companies compared to the American giants, they were very willing to culturally adapt to work in different cultural environments. As small companies they had to learn to work cooperatively with locals.

Now as a board member, day-to-day decisions on who the company should deal with were not part of my agenda. Nor did my personal feelings about Gaddafi factor into the equation. I believed in the company, and I wanted to see it succeed. With Libya on a new path—and the "mad dog" Gaddafi thought to be a thing of the past—the decision to expand there made good business sense, not only for SNC-Lavalin, but also for many global companies.

SNC-Lavalin also had an advantage: Riadh Ben Aissa.

* * *

Born and raised in Tunisia, Riadh Ben Aissa moved to Canada and ultimately gained both an undergraduate business degree and his MBA from the University of Ottawa. After graduating, he ran a small consulting firm that specialized in issuing studies on developing economies. His ex-wife, Marianne Vezina, told *La Presse* many years later that Riadh "had ambition, he was very motivated to do good things in his life."

In 1985, Lavalin acquired his company and he joined the firm. Initially confined to selling services in North Africa and the Middle East, Ben Aissa's breakthrough came two years later, when he received a phone call from Marcel Dufour, one of Lavalin's co-owners. "I hear that you are a capable Tunisian," Dufour told the young marketer. By the next day Ben Aissa was back in his native country, persuading a client to drop a $3-million lawsuit and to give Lavalin an extension on the contract.

His early years with Lavalin and then SNC-Lavalin were impressive. He acquired his fireman status by fixing difficult problems, and in 1988 as a young thirty-year-old, he was appointed regional director for the Middle East and North Africa. He helped win a very large contract for a subway system in Turkey in 1988. His biggest win was the Great Man-Made River Project in 1995, an audacious plan to pump water from immense underground aquifers in southern Libya to populated coastal areas in the north.

His performance record won him the position of executive vice-president of the infrastructure division, the firm's largest and most profitable. In that capacity he mined various Middle East and North African countries—Saudi Arabia, Turkey, Algeria, Tunisia and others—for the most massive projects imaginable—airports, bridges, canals, railroads, hospitals, mass transit systems, and more, all with budgets typically measured in hundreds of millions of dollars.

Ben Aissa was both respected and feared by many in the company. One executive who spoke anonymously to the *Globe and Mail* said that he had learned that one of Riadh's relatives was a shareholder in SNC-Lavalin's Saudi subsidiary and when he told a colleague he got a warning: "Don't you dare badmouth or lay a finger on this guy Ben Aissa." Ben Aissa had built his own empire inside the company.

Success followed success, boosting not only Ben Aissa's status within SNC-Lavalin but his lifestyle. By 2011, according to press coverage years later, he owned properties in Paris, Monaco, and Switzerland, and travelled frequently between Montreal, Tunisia, and Libya. He owned three flats in Residence du Parc Saint Roman, an exclusive apartment next to the Monte Carlo Country Club with stunning views of the Mediterranean. Had we known about his extensive real estate holdings at the time, we would certainly have wondered where the money was coming from.

Perhaps better than anyone at SNC-Lavalin, he thrived in the company's eat-what-you-kill, hunter-style culture, running his own show and reaping the benefits. It was a symbiotic relationship. So long as his values and goals aligned with the company's, this independence was a big win for everyone.

The work he did required a certain degree of confidence and swagger—knowing who to talk to, how to talk to them, and how to open doors and navigate places unfamiliar to most Canadian executives.

Stories about his style and his successes circulated throughout the company. Some SNC-Lavalin executives credited him with single-handedly landing a lucrative contract with Aramco, Saudi-Arabia's state-run oil company. Scoring a win that large, in an environment so closed and demanding, required building trust and relationships over years—saying the right things to the right people at the right time.

Those skills would be essential to win business in Libya, where all roads inevitably led to the erratic and volatile Gaddafi and his sons.

Riadh certainly built strong relationships with Saadi and Saif Gaddafi, sons of the Libyan leader. He sponsored a Gaddafi soccer club in Tripoli and assisted with a 2005 exhibition of Saif Gaddafi's paintings in Montreal, which was panned by critics. The strength of his relationship with Saadi is revealed in a 2009 email that he sent to Saadi, "My dear friend, make sure that this project will be ours. We have the best offer. I count on you."

When Ben Aissa first forayed into the Libya market, he reported to the company that he had found an agent to help him navigate the ins and outs of doing business there. This was common practice. Agents acted much like freelance sales and marketing people in foreign markets where a company lacked a large, on-the-ground presence.

In this case, Ben Aissa said the agent, whose name had to remain confidential, wanted to be paid under their company's name into a Swiss account, according to Larouche's *La Saga SNC-Lavalin.* This would be the first time the name Duvel would be logged into SNC-Lavalin's books.

My focus in this book is the period 2011 to 2019 (the years of the SNC-Lavalin scandal covered extensively in the press). I have been asked what the former CEO, Jacques Lamarre, knew. I cannot say one way or the other whether Jacques knew that Ben Aissa and Bebawi (who had been succeeded by Ben Aissa) were paying bribes to the Gaddafis.

Perhaps others with more of the facts can answer that conclusively. I do know that the authorities, who have significantly more information about the prior period than I do, decided not to lay charges against Jacques.

I am, however, certain that Jacques did not know that Bebawi and Ben Aissa were taking money for themselves from the company. Ben Aissa claimed that Jacques knew what was happening but given Jacques' proprietary attitude to the company, I doubt that this was true. He thought of SNC-Lavalin as his family business and would never have accepted someone stealing from the company. "If I had known," Jacques told *La Presse* in 2019 about Riadh's theft, "I would have shown him the door with a kick to the backside."

I also believed Jacques side of the story because of an incident that happened a few years before. As the chairman of the human resource committee, I met with him each year to discuss the bonuses that would be paid to the company's executives. The only time I had a heated conversation with him about the bonuses was a year where he felt that we should pay Bebawi double what the company's formula would have suggested. Jacques was adamant that we should override the company's policy. He and I discussed the topic so fervently that we were thirty minutes late for the board dinner being held that night at the Mount Royal Club.

It seems far-fetched to me to believe that Jacques would have argued for so long for an extra $100,000 for Bebawi if he was aware that Bebawi was simultaneously stealing millions from the company. Compared to what Sami was actually taking, the $100,000 would have seemed like a rounding error.

And Ben Aissa, for all his success, did not have an entirely clean bill of health with the company and the board. After Saadi's trip to Canada in 2008 and 2009 we discovered that Ben Aissa had spent millions to entertain him in Montreal and Toronto, shelling out thousands of dollars on Beluga caviar and Cristal Champagne. The company had even footed the bill to decorate Saadi's Toronto condo.

During the trip, Saadi also left a trail of expensive bills that SNC executives swooped in to pay. Stéphane Roy would later testify, "Saadi and his entourage would go to a restaurant on Saturday night with no credit cards and no cash, nothing to pay with. And they'd leave the place, and I'd receive a panicked call [from another executive] telling me 'Deal with that. Pay, pay, pay.'"

Saadi was meant to be in town for education. Lamarre gave him a presentation on leadership. Philippe Couillard, then Quebec's health minister, also gave a lecture to Saadi. "I quickly realized he was not very interested," he told *Le Devoir*. (Saadi was also entertained dogsledding in my hometown of Chibougamau.) When Saadi finally departed Canada, Lamarre was relieved, but also angry. He had stuck SNC-Lavalin with bills of close to $2 million.

"Everybody was so mad," Lamarre told a reporter at the time. "The board was mad. Everybody was really, really unhappy about that $2 million. At the end of the day what do we do? We did pay it. But we were very unhappy about that."

Hosting an event for a client who was in town, as SNC-Lavalin had done for Saadi, was entirely reasonable. But this amount was not reasonable. Many companies have large entertainment budgets. They might choose to entertain important clients at the Toronto International Film Festival or at the Masters golf tournament. When I was CEO of Pep Boys, the US automotive service chain, I was often invited to events by our largest suppliers who were trying to build stronger relationships with us. As an investor in a few private equity funds, I have attended many events put on by companies. One year I was in Santa Barbara for an all-expenses paid three-day meeting that included John Cougar Mellencamp singing for 150 of us. All companies do this but what Ben Aissa and his underlings had done was of a different order of business entirely.

When I was deposed in my role as chairman in a shareholder class action case, I learned some $30,000 had been spent on sex workers in addition to nights out at the infamous Wanda's strip club in downtown Montreal.

Jacques promised that Ben Aissa would be told his spending was unacceptable, and he later reported back that it had been done. I sometimes wonder if we did the right thing. With the benefit of hindsight, I now believe that we should have called Riadh Ben Aissa in to hear directly from us about the board's dissatisfaction with his lavish spending. We should have also used the opportunity to clarify acceptable client entertainment budgets and activities with everyone in the Office of the President. That would have sent a much clearer message to Ben Aissa and to his peers.

But I trusted Jacques. He was an honorable leader who lived and breathed SNC-Lavalin. His brother had been CEO and his son, Patrick, was a successful executive in the company. Whatever was happening under Jacques' watch, he would not have tolerated someone taking even a cent away from the business. I strongly believed this then and still do today.

We assumed that he did what needed to be done to resolve the issue. All of us, though, seem to have underestimated Ben Aissa and how far he would go.

4 | The Eagle Scout

There are different views as to how boards and CEOs should interact. Boards represent the shareholders and are responsible for governance and oversight, for making sure that a CEO is kept within certain guardrails. But when the board takes its mandate too far, it can end up meddling in the management of a company.

When I was CEO of Chapters, for example, a board member once quizzed me on why we'd decided to place a store location on one side of a street versus the other. That wasn't helpful. It was an operating management decision, not the board's. My team had studied the location for months. If you really want to know the answer to that, I explained to the director, I can arrange for you speak with our head of real estate. In my view, directors should abide by the "nose in and fingers out" mantra.

At the other extreme, a board can give a CEO very wide latitude to run the company. Gwyn Morgan, having himself been a successful CEO, was firmly in this camp. He'd run a very complex business, heading up Canada's largest energy company, EnCana Corp.

As a chairperson, I count on a CEO to be an honest person. When that trust is breached, as happened under Pierre, the relationship is over. I strongly believed that Pierre had to step down.

I am sure my thinking was influenced by my background in the military, where the rules are crystal clear: commanders are responsible for all actions taken by those under their authority. In the navy, the captain of any ship that runs aground is relieved of command, even if they were asleep or not on the bridge when it occurred. That's the hard and fast rule. There are no appeals.

When soldiers in my former unit, the Canadian Airborne Regiment, killed young Somalis, the commanding officer was relieved of command. He did not commit the crime, but it happened on his watch. In more recent news, Israel's military chief of staff, Lieutenant-General Herzi Halevi, resigned over the military's failure to prevent the October 7 Hamas attack. Those in command must take responsibility for the actions of the people under them.

This kind of military protocol may sound too strict and inflexible for civilian life, but it's very good at delineating responsibility. Duhaime was the captain of SNC-Lavalin, and on his watch the company had lost substantial funds, and a level of public confidence that threatened to cripple the company. That, and under his stewardship, two senior executives had left under a cloud of serious suspicion.

I was reminded also of the Royal Military College motto, which had been ingrained into us at the school: "Truth, Duty, Valour." I found it frustrating that a person at that most senior level would be, frankly, lying to the board—and worse, that he seemed to believe that the truth wouldn't eventually come out.

As one director put it to me: "The senior management team had set up an elaborate system of deceit and hiding."

Again, military protocol offers some hard and fast rules: if you've done something wrong or don't understand something, you admit it, immediately. Failing to do so sets off a cascade of worsening problems.

Pierre Duhaime had stepped into very big shoes when he assumed the CEO role three years earlier—Jacques was viewed everywhere as one of the country's best large company leaders. In 2002, his smiling face had appeared on the cover of the then-influential *Canadian Business* magazine next to the caption, "Meet Canada's Best CEO."

Choosing his successor at SNC-Lavalin had been a year-long process, carried out with immense attention to detail.

Pierre had a degree in metallurgical engineering and an MBA from HEC, he had joined SNC-Lavalin in 1989 after spending several years with Noranda. Lamarre had tapped him to run the Industrial Division, where he scored several successes. Later he was moved to Mining And Metallurgical, the weakest division in the company back in 2001.

Mining is a tough business, operating in some of the toughest environments in the world. In the ten years before he became CEO, Pierre probably logged the most travel miles of any executive in the company. By 2008, thanks to Pierre's leadership, the Mining And Metallurgical Division had emerged as the company's strongest performer. The people who worked for him thought he walked on water.

He also enjoyed the confidence of many directors. "He's tenacious and has a solid reputation with clients," board member David Goldman said publicly in assessing him. As part of the CEO selection process I, as the chair of the HR committee, had one-on-one meetings with each member of the office of the president to solicit their views on the potential CEO candidates.

I didn't, then or now, believe that Pierre Duhaime was the mastermind behind the payments to shell companies. When he assumed the CEO chair, Riadh Ben Aissa had been running his own show for some time. He was also comfortable in a corner of the world with which Pierre had limited familiarity. It made sense that Pierre would cut Ben Aissa a good deal of slack, treating him with kid gloves lest the Tunisian superstar throw a tantrum and take his talents, contacts, and money-making skills elsewhere.

I also suspect now that Duhaime—dropped into an extremely tough job and company culture—was intimidated by Ben Aissa. There was a time when Ben Aissa was considered a contender to be the next CEO.

In turn, Ben Aissa likely knew his value to the firm and took full advantage of the freedom from oversight he enjoyed under this new CEO. Would a stronger-spined CEO have gone in and pulled apart Ben Aissa's division to get to the bottom of what was going on? It's easy to second guess now, but I think they would have.

On March 26 the company put out a press release saying that Pierre Duhaime had stepped down and that Ian Bourne would take his place as interim CEO. Ian, along with Gwyn Morgan, Claude Mongeau, and I, would form a search committee to find the next CEO.

The press release also outlined in detail the results so far of our investigation, which had found $56 million in irregular payments. Critically, the release noted the payments were being reported to the police and that the company would cooperate fully with any investigation.

* * *

Ian Bourne stepped in as interim CEO while we searched for a permanent replacement. His business experience and his integrity outweighed any shortcomings he had in the engineering sector.

Ian set out straight away to introduce tough new standards of conduct and tighter internal controls They were badly needed. Everyone associated with the company was still in shock over the recent problems. And the reverberations would continue over the coming months.

His moves provided much-needed stability and gave the company's employees, suppliers, clients, and indeed the market generally, confidence.

As a first order of business, we decided to gather the top 120 executives for a management committee meeting at a large hotel in Montreal. We gave the attendees a board report on the situation and gave them an opportunity to ask questions about the crisis.

Some employees and some public commentators felt that we had been too generous in the severance package for Pierre. Later that year, the board learned that Pierre had been charged by authorities. Thus, on December 13 a press release was issued stating that "this development suggests there may be additional facts regarding Mr. Duhaime of which the Board was not aware at the time of his departure. Accordingly, the Board of Directors has decided to suspend the payments provided for under Mr. Duhaime's previously announced departure arrangements."

We had made clear to the authorities that we would cooperate fully with them. So, it came as a nasty surprise one morning in April—on a Friday the 13, fittingly—when the RCMP, press in tow, staged a raid on the SNC-Lavalin head office with no warning. Two RCMP officers had also travelled to Mexico to interview Cynthia Vanier. They told the CBC they spent a day asking her questions, mostly focused on Ben Aissa and Roy.

Ironically, at this exact time, the entire senior leadership of the company was off site at the Queen Elizabeth Hotel listening to a speech given by the CEO of Siemens Canada on how Siemens built a robust compliance culture after its bribery scandal.

We'd already invited the RCMP in, virtually rolled out a red carpet, and for optics-sake they decided to kick down the front door instead. Three weeks before this raid, on March 26, SNC-Lavalin had already handed over everything it had to the RCMP and the Sûreté du Québec.

The raid was cheap showboating in my opinion, but they were at least thoughtful enough to raid the offices on a Friday as they needed to take away many computers over the weekend.

The raid was widely covered by the press, which eagerly jumped on a "Mounties-get-their-man" story. Completely lost in the coverage was the fact that SNC-Lavalin had already reported what we knew to the police. One of the few beat reporters whom I felt was covering the story well and fairly was the *Globe and Mail*'s Konrad Yakabuski. Years after the raid I called him and complimented his work but noted, "You got it wrong when you said the company had not self-reported."

At a press conference after our annual general meeting that year, Gwyn Morgan sought to remind people of this point. Everything we'd found we had handed over to the Mounties. "Our hope is they have the capability and the means to go much further and much deeper," he said.

A few days of bad headlines were embarrassing. But this incident would haunt us in the coming years, fueling an unwarranted narrative that the company had not been open and cooperative from the outset.

That same week, Riadh Ben Aissa was arrested and jailed in Switzerland. Swiss investigators said it was part of a corruption, fraud, and money-laundering investigation in North Africa that began back in May 2011. They had been tracing funds that Ben Aissa had been funneling through Swiss accounts to Saadi Gaddafi. We'd uncovered $56 million in misattributed funds, but their investigation eventually alleged a total of $139 million.

Swiss officials outlined how money had been moved from SNC-Lavalin accounts to Swiss accounts controlled by Ben Aissa to accounts controlled by Saadi Gaddafi. They also detailed Saadi's spending, noting some of the money he received had been used to purchase a forty-six-meter super yacht named *Hokulani*, Hawaiian for "heavenly star."

The RCMP told the *Globe and Mail* that they had "received a request for assistance" from the Swiss in the case. This meant that the RCMP had been informed about the unauthorized payments *before* the company reported them—and before we even knew about them. It is fair to say that we didn't know what we didn't know.

It's notable that in the Swiss investigation SNC-Lavalin was considered one of the injured parties—a victim. Thanks to the Swiss, Ben

Aissa was forced to return $16.3 million of the money he stole to SNC Lavalin.

We could not have known about secret numbered accounts. Those were beyond the purview of any company's investigation. We had uncovered unauthorized payments, but it took the forensic powers of the police to learn who controlled the shell companies. The criminal here was Ben Aissa, but in Canada authorities were much more interested in going after the company rather than the individuals who stole the money.

Nevertheless, the RCMP had launched an investigation into SNC-Lavalin's dealings in Libya called Project Assistance. Any illusions that we board members had that only Riadh Ben Aissa would wear this were shattered. SNC-Lavalin was in hot water and would almost certainly be facing charges of some kind.

* * *

We tried to push the raid into the background and keep moving the company forward. We were once again on the hunt for a new CEO. Ian masterfully kept the vessel afloat while we searched for someone to take his place.

But finding someone with the skills and experience to not just manage a multi-billion-dollar, multi-national engineering firm but do it in the midst of crisis was a tall order. We were looking for an exceptional individual. We needed not only a seasoned engineering and construction executive, but someone widely regarded as an ethical leader. They could not have a single blemish on their record.

Everything had to take second place to finding and selecting someone who, as one member of the committee put it, would play the role of Eagle Scout in restoring SNC-Lavalin. (An eagle scout is the top rank in the Boy Scouts of America.) There were maybe a handful of people in the world who fit the bill.

We found a few outstanding candidates in Europe and the US. One stood out. Robert Card was leading a massive engineering project building venues for the 2012 London Olympics. He had previously overseen the decommissioning of the Rocky Flats nuclear weapons plant in Colorado. He was clearly no stranger to high-stakes, high-pressure jobs.

Card grew up on a farm in Yakima, Washington, obtained a civil engineering degree from the University of Washington and a master of science degree at Stanford. After rising to CEO of a Denver-based global engineering company, he served for three years as undersecretary of energy in Washington, DC, managing an annual budget of $14 billion and 65,000 federal and contractor employees.

We'd found our Eagle Scout. Card agreed to move to Montreal, and to take French lessons. He bought $1 million in SNC-Lavalin common shares to show he had a stake in the game. In October 2012 he and his wife—also an engineer, with an MBA from Harvard—made the move.

He was introduced as the new CEO in a lengthy conference call with investors in October. His message: "I'm committed to ensuring that the company's social license to operate remains our top priority."

5 | Cleaning house

In late 2012 I was having near weekly meetings with human resources.

I'd been chair of the HR committee for going on ten years. Until this point, it had been a pretty straightforward job. Among the main roles of an HR committee is to approve compensation for the CEO and his direct reports. And weigh in on the hiring and departures of senior executives.

Until Robert Card, we'd never hired a member of the office of the president from outside the company. When someone retired, it was well planned a year in advance who in the company was ready to step up and take their place. We'd also, of course, never had a whistle-blower complaint or scandals like the ones we had now, around Riadh Ben Aissa.

Card embraced his mission for ultimate transparency and set out to clean house. He was furiously hiring and firing, and I was signing off on the changes.

"On my second day I met with the top two hundred people in Montreal and just listened," Card told me. "They basically said what they wanted me to do and that was the exact plan I had come in with. Clean this up fast and let's get back to building things we are proud of." Card was impressed, overall, with the quality of the employees at SNC-Lavalin and thought they would have been successful in any large global engineering and construction business.

To clean house, Card eventually parted company with the head of international, our CFO, and several other executives. Most of those who were forced out were not proven to be part of the misdeeds that had been uncovered. But we felt they were in a position where they should have known about the payments of tens of millions of dollars.

This was certainly the case for the CFO, Gilles Laramee. Had he had strong relationships with the finance directors of every division, I don't think Ben Aissa would have gotten away with what he did. Stéphane Roy, Ben Aissa's finance director, would have gone straight to the CFO and said, "I'm being asked to do something very shady.' This didn't happen but should have.

These were tough decisions. "I felt terrible that we had to part ways with the CFO, who was a very nice guy and would have never been caught in this affair if he had been somewhere else," said Card.

I also was very fond of Gilles Laramee. I reached out to him just before his departure. I knew he was down about having to leave the company. He had grown up in the business and loved SNC-Lavalin. I suspect Gilles thought he could survive and be able to stay. We met for a drink at the Hotel Bonaventure in Montreal. It was a very emotional meeting. He was a good man, and I honestly felt sorry that he'd been placed in this difficult position.

Card's reorganization brought in some fresh faces. Neil Bruce had run operations for the London-based AMEC, a chief SNC-Lavalin rival. From London, Bruce would run a newly formed Resources and Environment Division, the company's biggest and most important. Bruce was clearly Robert Card and the board's chosen CEO-in-waiting.

Andreas Pohlmann was brought in as the chief compliance officer, a role that hadn't existed before. Compliance departments exist in financial institutions but are uncommon elsewhere. Pohlmann came from Siemens, where he'd set up a corporate governance program after the German engineering giant had been caught in the granddaddy of all corporate bribery scandals. It had paid $1.4 billion in bribes around the world and had to pay even more than that in fines when it was uncovered.

Bruce was a headline-grabbing hire, but Pohlmann was meant to send an equally strong message about SNC's priorities. We gave Pohlmann money and resources. He was among the highest paid execs at the company and set about building what would become a fifty-person compliance department—unheard of for an engineering and construction firm.

Within two years of Card's arrival, all but one of the people who directly reported to him had been replaced. "The amount of rebuilding we had to do was amazing," he said.

Card's commitment to righting the ship proved to be more aggressive than the position of many board members. For example, he felt that if there were any countries in the world where we could potentially get into further issues like we had in Libya, we were not going to operate there. That meant walking away from a lot of business, which naturally caused some nervousness. But we'd wanted an Eagle Scout and we'd got one.

Card had been hired to stabilize SNC-Lavalin, and in addition to the internal fixes he had to stickhandle what was a growing public perception crisis. The earthquake of bad news that had started rumbling the year before began shaking SNC-Lavalin in all directions when Quebec's anti-corruption squad arrested Pierre Duhaime in late November 2012 at his home in Montreal. He was facing fifteen charges including fraud, conspiracy and forgery. Also charged was Riadh Ben Aissa, still in prison in Switzerland since his arrest in April.

The charges against Pierre dated back to a 2007 bid on a contract to build a new $1.3-billion hospital in Montreal. SNC-Lavalin didn't have a lot of experience building hospitals, but at the time we felt a project of this size in our home city was something we should compete for aggressively. Again, we had badly underestimated what "aggressive" meant to Ben Aissa and, apparently, Duhaime. The RCMP accused Ben Aissa of paying a $22.5-million bribe to win the contract in 2010, with Duhaime's approval.

This was the mysterious third payment highlighted in a yellow folder that Stéphane Roy had handed over on the day he was fired. SNC-Lavalin's auditors had flagged the payment in their investigation but had been unable to identify what it related to. Ben Aissa claimed it was a gas project in Algeria.

The police now knew: Ben Aissa orchestrated the transfer of the money from SNC-Lavalin to a Bahamas-based company called Sierra Asset Management. That had been set up by Arthur Porter, at the time the chief executive of the McGill University Health Centre and chief negotiator of the new hospital contract.

A few months after Duhaime's initial arrest, police issued an arrest warrant for Porter. The fact that then-Prime Minister Stephen Harper had appointed Porter to the government's Security Intelligence Review Committee in 2008 and made him chair in 2010 had opposition politicians and the media buzzing with excitement at the time of the charges. A *Montreal Gazette* headline dubbed the case "The biggest fraud in Canadian history."

Pierre spent a day in detention before being released at 7:30 p.m. the evening of his arrest. It would be the start of his years-long legal battle. Porter had by this point left Montreal for the Bahamas and would never face justice in Canada. In 2013 he was arrested on an international warrant in Panama. A former oncologist, he died that year in a Panama City hospital of lung cancer.

At the same time as Duhaime's headline-grabbing arrest, the Charbonneau Commission, launched in October 2011 by the Liberal government of Jean Charest, was busy examining allegations of widespread corruption in the Quebec construction industry. The rest of Canada watched this unfold and was left with one pretty obvious conclusion: Quebec construction companies were corrupt. And they were not wrong. It was a black mark—deservedly so—for SNC-Lavalin and several other Quebec-based engineering companies, including Genivar (which renamed itself WSP Global in the wake of the scandal).

The big test of Card's strategy, and our commitment to it, arrived in June 2012 when the World Bank accused SNC-Lavalin of bribery in a bridge project in Bangladesh. Like the utterly unexpected cases of Vanier and Ben Aissa, it felt as though we'd been hit on the side of the head by a brick.

The Padma bridge project was a $3-billion, six-kilometer-long road and rail bridge—the largest in Bangladesh. SNC-Lavalin had bid on the $50-million construction contract. We landed on a shortlist of five companies, but didn't win.

The World Bank's integrity unit had received tips that so-called project consultancy costs (PCCs) paid by two SNC-Lavalin employees in Bangladesh were actually bribes intended to improve the company's standing in the bidding process. "PCC is a euphemism used by SNC-Lavalin to indicate the cost of the bribes to be paid," wrote the chairman of the World Bank panel looking into the allegations. They passed their information on to the RCMP, which led to charges in Canada against three former employees.

The stakes of the case were enormous. The World Bank imposed a settlement that would bar the company from bidding on projects that had World Bank financing for ten years. This was a severe penalty. For Robert Card's clean-up effort, this was a case of one-step forward, two steps back.

* * *

We had doubts about the veracity of the World Bank's accusations. The amount of money involved was small—just $10,000—and the charges seemed flimsy. Consultancy costs, like agents' fees, are standard business practice for any large company operating internationally. Where a firm doesn't have a large local presence, it hires agents and consultants, who have local relationships and expertise navigating local bureaucracies. Whether or not the World Bank had uncovered something nefarious here, it was not some kind of company-wide secret plot to disguise bribes.

Nevertheless, it was true that in countries with poor transparency rankings and where corruption is a fact of life, these consultancy costs or agents' fees can present a challenge, and companies can find themselves walking a fine line between what's acceptable and what's not.

In the late 1990s and early 2000s attitudes around bribery were changing quickly. The OECD had been pushing for an international convention, which would eventually come in to force in 1999, obliging all members states to have laws making it a crime for their citizens or companies to bribe foreign public officials. Canada put a foreign bribery law on the books in 1998, with the Corruption of Foreign Public Officials Act. And in 2008 the RCMP established an international anti-corruption unit.

Before this shift, in some western countries bribes would outright appear on company books as a normal cost of business. It wasn't until 2017 that Canada removed an exception in its corruption act that allowed facilitation payments, which it described as "payments made to foreign government officials to speed up or facilitate routine transactions such as permits."

Around the world, companies in the early 2000s were just beginning to take closer looks at the agents' fees they were paying. SNC-Lavalin was no exception.

The laws were changing faster than some companies' corporate cultures could keep up with. While bribery was being outlawed, it was still (and remains to this day) widespread. The World Bank estimates that each year, individuals and businesses pay $1 trillion in bribes, at a cost to global gross domestic product of $2.6 trillion.

Unfortunately, not all of our global competitors believe that bribery is wrong. That currently seems to be the case in the US. In *A Very Stable Genius*, President Donald Trump is quoted as saying in his first term in office, “It is so unfair that American companies aren’t allowed to pay bribes to get business overseas.” He went on to say that it was a “horrible law” and said that “the world is laughing at us.” On February 10, 2025, President Trump signed an executive order suspending the enforcement of the Foreign Corrupt Practices Act. The White House official website in February 2025 stated that “overexpansive and unpredictable FCPA enforcement against American citizens and businesses for routine business practices in other nations . . . actively harms American economic competitiveness and, therefore, national security.” This is not the view in most western nations, and I suspect that most US companies will continue to abide by the FCPA despite the fact that it will not be enforced for the next few years. Ironically many of the FCPA actions have been against non-US companies.

When is a bribe a bribe? The size of a payment is one of the most obvious ways to differentiate between a fee and a bribe. A $1-million commission on a $5-billion contract does not raise eyebrows. A $1-million commission on a $5-million contract means something is off. Although, in reality, large cases of bribery are not so easy to discern. As we had just painfully discovered at SNC-Lavalin, they can be well hidden behind shell companies and complex arrangements. They might even have management approval. In 2014 the OECD studied 427 large-scale bribery cases and found that in forty-one percent of the cases, corporate managers approved of the employee’s using bribery. In twelve percent, the CEO knew about or even approved the bribes.

Anyone who has traveled in some of the less-transparent countries in the world will know that bribery is a fact of life there. Back in the mid-1980s, I went to Prague, in then Czechoslovakia for a weekend and wound up detained for more than four hours before I was able to enter the country. What was clear to me was that the customs official wanted me to pay him some money. These officials were not highly paid, and this was how they were able to make ends meet. Being stubborn I was unwilling to pay. Eventually, after a four hour wait, my persistence paid off when there was a shift change, and the next customs officials let me in.

In the case of Ben Aissa in Libya, Swiss investigators found that from 2001 to 2011, $118 million was transferred from SNC-Lavalin to Duvel Securities Inc. and a second company Dinova International Inc, which were used to funnel money to Saadi Gaddafi and to accounts held by Ben Aissa and Sami Bebawi, who had headed up SNC-Lavalin's Construction Division until 2006. These companies were not joint ventures, but rather tools to hide bribes. Ben Aissa was listed as the sole owner of Duvel, as well as Dinova International Inc. In total, more than $73 million went through the companies to Ben Aissa and Bebawi, according to Canadian prosecutors.

Even with the help of forensic accountants, SNC-Lavalin had no way to trace where the money had ended up. All we could tell is that funds had gone to offshore accounts at various banks in the Caribbean or numbered companies and were billed to accounts where work had not been done. This billing to different projects was done to hide these amounts. We had no legal authority to get a bank to open its books for us. Only police investigators, with subpoenas and threats of criminal charges, could get inside the Caribbean banks and uncover the true details.

These cases were theft and bribery writ large. Ben Aissa was both moving funds to Saadi Gaddafi and pocketing money himself.

The World Bank's accusation against SNC-Lavalin centered on a payment of around $10,000. Not a small amount, but also not the kind of money that influences a $50-million contract. This was, in the grand scheme, a petty cash amount for country managers. They would not have been raised at the division level of the company, let alone the corporate level.

In light of this, the ten year-ban we were facing seemed way immensely harsh. It would be the longest disbarment that the World Bank had ever given, and this for an unproven bribery case involving $10,000.

Card felt we were being singled out by the World Bank at a time when it was eager to show it was cracking down on bribery. A Canadian company already embroiled in a high-profile bribery scandal was an easy target.

As well, Ottawa was unwilling to step in and help. The fact that SNC-Lavalin was one of Canada's biggest, most important companies, which had helped build everything from Montreal's Olympic Stadium to Vancouver's Canada Line to Newfoundland's Hibernia oil platform and was a source of pride (at least in Quebec), didn't seem to mean anything.

I'm quite sure had SNC-Lavalin been an American company, the secretary of state and probably the president would have been on the line with the World Bank to say, "Yeah, we're not accepting this." The French, Germans, British, and Japanese would have done the same. As we'd soon find, Canada had a different view.

One option was to continue to fight the World Bank charges. The other course of action, which Bob Card was strongly urging, was to settle the case and move on. We'd be reinforcing the image that SNC-Lavalin was a new company, ready and willing to put anything with a whiff of impropriety behind it. And with the weight of the Duhaime arrest, the Ben Aissa revelations, and the ongoing Charbonneau commission pressing down on us, we were hardly on solid footing for a fight.

Card stressed that even if the company had done nothing wrong, fighting the charges could take years, and become a big, ugly obstacle to his turnaround efforts. He'd been clear when he joined as CEO that his rebuilding plan was a three- or four-year undertaking, not six or seven.

I was swayed by Bob's thinking as were enough other board members. We signed off on the Eagle Scout's plan, though it would remain a point of contention. Export Development Canada (EDC), meanwhile, decided that if the World Bank put us in the penalty box, it should as well. Card and I visited EDC to plead our case to try to have the decision reversed to no avail. Fortunately, the EDC ban didn't last more than a year.

One of the main conditions that the World Bank placed on SNC-Lavalin was that it would install a monitor inside the company to keep tabs on us. Joseph Covington was a Washington lawyer who in the 1980s had headed up the US Department of Justice's Foreign Corrupt Practices Act Unit. Like Pohlmann, he was a star in his field. The World Bank was not messing around.

Every three or four months, Convington would make the trip to Montreal, where he had the run of SNC-Lavalin. He also checked in on projects overseas. He'd meet with the CEO, the board—talk to anyone he wanted to, sit in on any meeting he fancied, and pore over any financials he felt like. He had an enormous amount of power over us—a negative review from him would be a big setback in our efforts to move forward.

By this point I was chairing the governance committee, and so had regular meetings with Covington. I found him to be quite fair. He didn't drill us on small things and kept his focus on the main compliance issues. He was ultimately sympathetic to companies' struggles with foreign bribery, and to the view that they often do try to do the right thing when confronted with corruption.

On the subject of bribery, he wrote in 2011, "In my almost forty years of experience, I have rarely seen American companies affirmatively offering bribes in the first instance; rather they are typically reacting to a world not of their making."

"It is a fact that corruption in government remains endemic worldwide and that is not likely to change," he wrote. "As the world shrinks companies who seek to do the right thing can't help but confront corrupt officials—as customers, regulators, and adjudicators—and confront them often. The problem with current [US] laws and enforcement policies is that they do not adequately reward companies for sincere (and expensive) efforts to stop the unwanted misbehaviour of their employees."

Covington seemed generally impressed with Robert Card's efforts. At one point he told the company that "SNC-Lavalin has made great progress to remedy the problems of the past and by instituting solid procedures to prevent new problems." His reports to the World Bank were not made public, but having read them, I can say he was giving SNC-Lavalin high marks. Given his credibility, that had real value.

For all the trouble SNC-Lavalin faced, we felt that we had finally arrived at a pretty good spot. The company was being whipped into shape and shareholders were convinced we were on the right track. More than that, they seemed thrilled with the transparency that our new CEO had brought to the company. We could confidently say that, yes, we'd made some bad mistakes, but we'd also made dramatic changes to make sure they wouldn't happen again. (The World Bank would eventually lift the ban two years early because of the company's successful compliance efforts.)

Of course, we weren't entirely in the clear yet. Since the RCMP raid, we knew full well the company would still be held accountable for the Ben Aissa debacle. We were going to be in the penalty box. But we hoped and believed it would be a minor penalty, not a game misconduct. SNC-Lavalin had been proactive, taken its lumps and, given the conditions placed on us by the World Bank, was well along the path of remediation.

But how we'd dealt with the World Bank had effects that we did not anticipate. Not fighting it was about to become one of my chief regrets in this ordeal. While our investors were happy, there were others—Canadian public servants who would soon have real power over the fate of the company—who were eager to latch on to a completely different narrative. To Canadian federal prosecutors, that World Bank guilty plea was just proof that SNC-Lavalin was corrupt and irredeemable, no matter what it did.

6 | Deal, no deal

We had hoped to resolve the issue and make a deal with the federal government, but this did not happen. We could only speculate as to why. It seemed plausible that the Conservative government of the day, led by Stephen Harper, might not want to be seen doing a favor for a Quebec-based company. SNC-Lavalin was still squarely in the media spotlight, so the deal would certainly have attracted a lot of attention. And the coverage that had come from the World Bank case was not good. The message we had wanted to send was that we were taking our lumps and doing the right thing. Unfortunately, what most people would have taken from the headlines at the time was, "Boy, that must be one really bad company."

The company could not change the past but it was doing everything possible to make sure that the events would never occur again. We'd built a massive compliance department, unrivalled in our industry, welcomed a world-class World Bank monitor into the fold, and parted ways with anyone remotely connected to the troubles.

Ben Aissa had pleaded guilty in 2014 to the charges he was facing in Switzerland: fraud, corruption, and money laundering. He was sentenced to time served, twenty-nine months, and would be returned to Canada, where he would face charges over the Montreal hospital bid. SNC-Lavalin—again, an "injured party" in the case—stood to recover $16 million in funds seized from him.

The Quebec government was very supportive. As Quebec's minister of the economy Jacques Daoust said, "We can reproach SNC-Lavalin for things and we can have individuals who did reprehensible things, but the current enterprise is eminently correct. If we have three people who did reprehensible acts, and we affect 45,000 people, I think in a sense, we also have to respect that."

And that's exactly what a criminal charge against SNC-Lavalin would do; it was the equivalent of corporate capital punishment. In 2014, the Conservative government introduced an automatic ten-year debarment from federal contracting for convicted companies. SNC-Lavalin's business was based on large government infrastructure projects.. If we were to plead guilty, that would evaporate, and this would have dramatically impacted the company's business.

Robert Card had always assumed his Eagle Scout plan would yield a deal with the government. His view was at least somewhat informed by the fact that he was American. Because in the United States, his plan almost certainly would have worked.

Card understood how it might work in the United States but not here. He'd served as undersecretary of energy under a Republican administration. And in his experience, government was essentially business-friendly, and the US secretaries who ran departments tended to have business backgrounds. They were not, as is more often the case in Canada with federal ministers, career politicians.

In Canada, being anti-business is generally good politics. Politicians' attacking big banks, big telcos, and even big tech companies usually wins votes.

Bob had real difficulty seeing how unaligned the Canadian government was with the interests of one of its biggest, most important companies. Surely, he assumed, we're not going to get the death penalty for what we did given all the positive changes that had been made? There must be a way to sit across the table from reasonable government officials and come up with a plan to pay for what happened and move on.

The US and UK would never handle a case the way Canada was, he said. "They would have righted the ship immediately and they would have been partners in making that happen."

Writing for the Ottawa-based think-tank, the Public Policy Forum, Sean Speer, who was a senior economic adviser to Prime Minister Stephen Harper, explained the difference between the American and Canadian approaches. He noted that America's "political actors are motivated by a conception of national interest that views the commercial interests of its biggest companies as inextricable to the interests of America itself. Canadian politicians don't think that way. They might sign a letter supporting a bid of a Canadian company for a foreign contract. But they're not prepared to wield the levers of statecraft to defend and support their interests on the global stage."

Card later told me that the hardest part of his job at SNC-Lavalin was trying to explain to customers, both domestic and internationally, why the Canadian government was not on our side.

* * *

While the United States was clearly more interested in giving a hand-up to business, it was nevertheless ramping up a crackdown on foreign bribery, just like Canada. The USA's attitude to foreign bribery had been fairly lax before 2000. But things changed dramatically after the collapse of Enron in 2001 and the introduction of the Sarbanes-Oxley Act in 2002, which required public disclosure of material events including possible acts of foreign bribery.

In 2000, there were no prosecutions under the US Foreign Corrupt Practices Act (FCPA). Within a decade, the US had around 150 open FCPA cases. The US was taking these cases seriously. And prosecuting them had become a big business on its own. But unlike Canada, it was clear how the large majority of these cases would end: with a deferred prosecution agreement, or a DPA.

Any follower of Canadian news will, by now, be at least passingly familiar with the term DPA. Thanks to SNC-Lavalin, they were about to become a very hot topic in Canada. But at the time, they were a pretty ordinary and widely used tool in the US. And soon, elsewhere in the world: In the UK, a DPA regime came into effect in 2014. France and Australia would follow in 2016 and 2017, respectively.

A DPA is an agreement entered into between the prosecution and a company alleged to have committed crimes. It suspends—or defers—prosecution of the company while putting in place certain measures like fines, reporting requirements, and third-party oversight to ensure compliance (much like our World Bank monitor).

It's roughly the equivalent of a plea bargain for an individual who agrees on a certain penalty (fines, community service, probation) as an alternative to prison. If the person doesn't stick to the terms of their probation (like checking in with probation officers periodically) then that individual can still be sent to prison. The same goes for DPAs. If a company doesn't follow the terms, it can still be prosecuted.

The biggest misconception about DPAs—one that persists —is that they are get-out-of-jail-free cards. This is odd given that you cannot put a corporation, a legal entity, in jail and that DPAs certainly intend to punish the individual wrong doers. DPAs are actually designed to ensure companies are financially punished and clean up their act. Done right, they can be quite severe and effective. Much like prison is ineffective at reducing recidivism, simply prosecuting a company for a crime does not necessarily lead to reform—especially when the individuals

Companies that have benefitted from DPAs

who commit the crimes get off scot-free. DPA's also incentivize companies to voluntarily disclose misconduct—a precondition for getting such an agreement.

From the moment the Libya crisis emerged, DPAs had been part of our boardroom conversations. We knew no such law existed in Canada, but they were a pretty good model for what we hoped could happen. They made too much sense to ignore. But getting a law on the books in Canada would take too long. It didn't seem realistic, so we favored a plea deal.

While we tried to strike this deal with Ottawa, we watched as several large US and European companies benefited from DPAs.

There was, for instance, the French transportation giant Alstom in 2014. The US Justice Department found that Alstom had engaged in rampant bribery abroad to win power-generation deals. Over more than a decade, Alstom paid more than $75 million in bribes to secure $4 billion in projects in markets such as Indonesia, Egypt, Saudi Arabia, the Bahamas, and Taiwan. In Indonesia, for example, Alstom paid bribes to a high-ranking member of parliament and two executives of the state owned electricity company. All this bribery provided the company with more than $300 million in profits. Alstom was caught, pleaded guilty, and agreed to pay a $772-million fine.

Another French company, Alcatel, was charged with two counts of violating the US Foreign Corrupt Practices Act (FCPA) for paying bribes in Latin America and Asia. This telecom conglomerate paid $137 million in fines to settle the case. A Swedish telecommunications company, Telia Company AB, agreed to pay $965 million in 2017 for FCPA violations in Uzbekistan. Telia had paid $330 million to a shell company controlled by an Uzbek government official to win contracts in the country.

In the pharmaceutical industry alone, there was GSK (formerly Glaxo Smith Kline), which paid $3 billion in fines to settle allegations of health care fraud and bribery in 2012. Eli Lily had paid $1.4 billion in fines as punishment for hiding safety data and paying kickbacks to doctors. Merck in 2011, agreed to pay $950 million in fines for similar infractions. Before that, Johnson and Johnson paid fines to settle allegations of illegal marketing practices and for paying kickbacks to doctors. All of these firms were punished but able to carry on with their businesses.

Then there was the case of Pfizer. It managed to secure four DPAs in the U.S. In 2012 it paid $60.2 million to settle charges of violating the Foreign Corrupt Practices Act (FCPA) for bribing government officials in Bulgaria, Croatia, Kazakhstan, and Russia. The principal deputy assistant US attorney general, Mythili Raman, argued that "Pfizer took shortcuts to boost its business in several Eurasian countries, bribing government officials in Bulgaria, Croatia, Kazakhstan and Russia to the tune of millions of dollars."

According to the US Securities and Exchange Commission, Pfizer used various methods to conceal the bribes, including creating fake invoices and using third-party agents to secure contracts. In 2009, Pfizer paid $2.3 billion to settle charges of illegally promoting and paying kickbacks to doctors to prescribe Bextra. Pfizer also paid $75 million to settle a lawsuit for conducting illegal clinical trials that led to the deaths of several children.

This trail of wrongdoing is the cautionary tale of DPAs. Clearly, the reforms that were put in place at Pfizer didn't go far enough. I strongly believe that corporations that are hit with multiple offences should face increasingly severe penalties.

Pfizer also underscored one of the problems with DPAs, and really with the handling of corporate crime everywhere—the individuals behind the crimes were not being punished.

Nevertheless, in the case of Pfizer, despite its repeat offences, nobody thought it wise to destroy the company. And in this case, at least, we should be thankful that US regulators sought to punish, not decapitate it, for its wrongdoing. Pfizer was still in business to develop a miraculous COVID-19 vaccine, saving literally millions of lives.

At SNC-Lavalin, our thinking and actions were guided by the case of Siemens. The lessons Siemens had learned, passed along to us by our compliance officer Andreas Pohlmann, informed many of the steps we were taking under Card's leadership. When Canadian prosecutors would later say that what SNC-Lavalin had done was without precedent and thus it was not eligible for a DPA, they clearly had not heard of the Siemens case.

A large international engineering firm like SNC-Lavalin, Siemens had retained some 2,700 "consultants" whose job it was to pay foreign officials to win business. When the scandal broke, they were found to have made 4,283 corrupt payments, totaling $1.4 billion, in more than a dozen countries. The company had paid $100 million to Argentine officials to secure a $1-billion contract to create national identity cards. In Bangladesh it paid bribes to the son of the prime minister and to the minister of telecommunications, among others, to win the contract on a national telecommunications project. In Venezuela Siemens used kickbacks to win a $340 million railway system contract.

Siemens was also involved in bribing Greek government officials during the 2004 Summer Olympic Games in Athens. A *New York Times* 2008 headline captured the company's culture succinctly: "At Siemens bribery was just a line item." It is worth noting that before 1999 bribes were tax deductible as business expenses under the German tax code. Inside Siemens bribes were referred to as "NA," a German abbreviation for the phrase "*nutzliche Aufwendungen,*" which means useful money.

A mid-level Siemens executive, Reinhard Siekaczek, oversaw an annual bribery budget of between $40 and $50 million from 2002 until 2006. His job was to funnel payments to secret accounts to win important contracts. One such payment made by Siekaczek's group was for $12.7 million to senior government officials in Nigeria. "We thought we had to do it," he said. "Otherwise, we'd ruin the company."

(Siekaczek later cooperated with German authorities after his arrest in 2006 and was sentenced to two years probation and a $150,000 fine. He never believed that he was risking jail for doing what Siemens asked him to do. He was just the man in the middle.)

This was not a case of a few bad apples going behind the top executives' backs. In fact, when people outside Siemens started getting suspicious in late 2002 about these payments, five executives in the telecom group met in Munich to discuss how to better disguise them. Not only did Siemen's not self-report, but it also went out of its way to hide what it was doing.

As Joseph Persichini, the director of the FBI's Washington office said, "the Siemens bribery program was massive, willful and carefully orchestrated."

Working together, the Munich public prosecutors office and the US Department of Justice brought charges against Siemens in 2008. The company entered into a deferred prosecution agreement and was fined $1.6 billion, at the time the largest fine ever levied in a bribery case. That may seem like a lot, but for Siemens, with a little over $100 billion in revenue, it represented about 1.5 percent of its sales.

Notably, Siemens did not plead guilty to bribes which could have prohibited it from bidding on US or Canadian government contracts. Siemens also agreed to have a monitor in place for four years and the CEO resigned, although he claimed, as Pierre Duhaime had, that he was unaware of the bribery scheme. German authorities convicted two former Siemens employees and the US indicted six.

For the first time since its founding in 1847, Siemens hired a CEO, Peter Loscher, from outside the company. It also instituted a companywide compliance system. The new CEO replaced eighty percent of the top-level management. Again, a playbook we'd followed at SNC-Lavalin.

Siemens was a clear case where the DPA system worked. The guilty were punished—although I would argue that the most senior executives got off with a slap on the wrist. The company paid its fines and put a genuine compliance program in place, staffed by more than four hundred people. The culture at Siemens fundamentally changed.

Just as important, the German government did not try to destroy the company, which remains an important pillar in the nation's economy and continues to carry out big projects around the world. In 2018 Canada's VIA Rail signed a nearly $1-billion deal with Siemens to replace its fleet of trains on the busy Quebec-Windsor corridor.

It was hard not to look at the Siemens case and feel like, as a Canadian company, the playing field wasn't level. What would have happened to Siemens if it had been headquartered in Montreal? Instead of going to bat for us, Canada seemed set in its desire not to rehabilitate SNC-Lavalin, but only to pursue charges and punish us— the nuclear option.

Increasingly, we were struggling to understand how our decision to plead guilty in the World Bank case—and work with the monitor—wasn't earning us any credit with prosecutors. We weren't expecting sympathy. A number of SNC-Lavalin employees had committed crimes, including our former CEO. But the work we'd been doing to turn thing around just didn't seem to be registering.

Card and the World Bank monitor, Joe Covington, got on like a house on fire—the Eagle Scout and the Lawman. But the same could not be said for Chair Ian Bourne and Covington.

I was more and more sympathetic with Bourne's position. We had accepted a ten year-disbarment and a guilty plea that would come to haunt us down the road in our dealings with Canadian prosecutors.

The added sting would come in 2017, when Canadian charges over the Padma Bridge project fell apart—thrown out by a judge who ruled that it was based on sloppy police work. If we'd fought it, we would have won.

And of course, for any SNC-Lavalin CEO, comparisons with the beloved Jacques Lamarre were inevitable. How would Jacques, with his amazing business and political networks, have navigated this crisis?

Nevertheless, Bob Card was our CEO, and he had his mandate. Bob was also making big strides pushing the business forward. While much of his strategy was built around getting SNC out of the penalty box, he also set out to grow the company in some of the sectors where we were not particularly strong. He orchestrated the acquisition of the UK-based firm Kentz in 2014, making us a much bigger player in oil and gas.

Interestingly, the controversy swirling around SNC-Lavalin didn't slow the deal at all. While Canadians were bombarded with news about the company and its wrong doings, it was mostly a non-factor in Europe. I was having a casual conversation with the CEO of Kentz when it came up: How are you guys handling it? Is the worst if it behind you?

My answer to questions like this was that we're on the five-yard line. We're having discussions about getting a deal, and I think everybody sees the logic of why it is in nobody's interest to destroy the company.

It proved to be a naively optimistic answer. In February 2015 the charges we'd been fearing finally arrived. The Public Prosecution Service laid charges of fraud and corruption against SNC-Lavalin Group Inc., SNC-Lavalin International Inc., and SNC-Lavalin Construction Inc. They accused the company of paying $47.7 million in bribes and defrauding the Libyan government of $129.8 million.

The company put out a lengthy press release that summarized our view as politely as possible: "The charges stem from the same alleged activities of former employees from over three years ago in Libya, which are publicly known, and that the company has cooperated on with authorities since then. Even though SNC-Lavalin has already incurred significant financial damage and losses as a result of actions taken prior to March 2012, we have always been and remain willing to reach a reasonable and fair solution that promotes accountability, while permitting us to continue to do business and protect the livelihood of our over 40,000 employees, our clients, our investors and our other stakeholders."

The release also hinted at other countries' friendlier DPA regimes: "It is important to note that companies in other jurisdictions, such as the United States and United Kingdom, benefit from a different approach that has been effectively used in the public interest to resolve similar matters while balancing accountability and securing the employment, economic and other benefits of businesses."

We still held out some hope that a deal could be reached before this went to trial. But it was a long shot now. It was time to pivot. We suddenly faced the prospect of a path forward that once seemed impossible. To guarantee SNC-Lavalin's survival, we were going to have to change Canadian law.

7 | Looking for friends

A few weeks after the charges landed, the board asked me to step in to replace Ian Bourne as chairman. The problem with this plan was that I was planning my exit from the board as well. I believe in term limits for board members, and I'd been at SNC-Lavalin for fifteen years. Refreshing the board was just as important as the management shakeup the company had gone through. It was key that SNC-Lavalin present a new face under new leadership, top to bottom.

Those of us on the board couldn't entirely skirt responsibility for the corruption that had crept into the company under our watch. But I was convinced that we had done everything right. And it is virtually impossible for a board to prevent wrongdoing when it is orchestrated by a very few senior executives, especially if the CEO is one of them. The board isn't on site every day and has to leave the management of the company to the CEO and his team. When we found out what had happened in Libya, we took decisive action, firing the CEO, naming an interim team and hiring third-party forensic investigators to get the facts. I felt we'd gone above and beyond to make sure that the financial regulators and law enforcement, were fully informed at the same time that we were getting information.

Ultimately, I agreed to become chairman, at least for the short term.

In an environment where every tiny move SNC-Lavalin made was put under a microscope, the news went over reasonably well. The *Financial Post*'s coverage focused on my record as the founding CEO of Chapters and CEO of Pep Boys and on my military service. Diane Brisebois, the CEO of the Retail Council of Canada, offered some generous comments: "If there is anyone who personifies the expression

'The buck stops here,' who is going to take responsibility for whatever decision the team or its members has taken, it's Larry."

"I think what he brings is the courage to make the right decision," she added. "He will give people the courage to take the appropriate steps to grow the business and ensure the future of the business and its people."

Bruce Campbell, the president and portfolio manager at Campbell, Lee & Ross Investment Management and one of SNC-Lavalin's investors, told the *Financial Post* that my private-equity background at Bain made me the ideal chairman for the company's next phase, which included plans to sell its stake in the 407 highway. "If I had my wish list, [Mr. Stevenson] is the perfect guy for that," he said.

This rare bit of complimentary coverage offered me something of a honeymoon period.

I like to think all of the compliments were true, but my appeal to SNC-Lavalin, in addition to my good relationships inside the company, was that I also got along well with some of our biggest shareholders, like Michael Sabia, the CEO of Quebec's pension agency the Caisse de Dépôt et Placement du Québec. Sabia not only created enormous value for Quebec pensioners, but he also helped build Quebec's global champions. His staunch support for SNC-Lavalin would soon prove to be life-saving.

My first order of business—literally within minutes of being named chair in March 2015—was to call Bob Card. I told him I was stepping in as chair and asked if he'd fly to Toronto to meet with me.

Four hours later we were sitting in Canoe, a swanky downtown restaurant, along with fellow board director Alain Rheaume, who chaired the HR committee. Rheaume was in town for the board meeting and was staying overnight, so I suggested he join us.

I told Bob that we, Alain and I, speaking for the board, were supportive of him and his role with the World Bank monitor. He was our CEO. But he had to know there were concerns that the monitor was having too much of an influence.

We also had to discuss the succession plan. Card's hope all along had been that he'd come in, reform SNC-Lavalin, get a deal, and get out. We both knew that that timeline was now compromised. Bob and I agreed it was time to start planning his exit. The exact timing would be worked out in the coming months, but we'd start the search process for the next CEO. We hammered out the rough game plan: we'd consider two internal candidates and do a below-the-radar external search to compare them with the best outsiders.

I was happy with the outcome, and that Bob and I were on the same page. He had done the heavy diplomatic and compliance lifting. But after being in survival mode for so long, the Board thought we needed more of an operator—someone who could really focus on the business of engineering and construction.

The CEO of an engineering company is constantly placing "bets" on projects that will either be a hit, or a disaster six or seven years out. Under- or over-bidding on massive public works projects or mismanaging them could cost us billions. In my time at SNC-Lavalin, we'd only had one disastrous miss like that: the Goreway gas-fired power plant project in Brampton, Ontario, in 2007. (A key supplier in the construction project went bankrupt, causing a cascade of delays and ultimately huge losses.)

I was always uncomfortable with a CEO placing those bets but not being around to see them through. We were bidding, for instance, on the new Champlain bridge in Montreal. The person who was going to have to live with that was the next CEO, not Bob Card.

Within a few months of our dinner, we had the details sorted and the succession plan ready.

Neil Bruce had come to SNC-Lavalin knowing he was our leading candidate to be the next CEO. He'd been told, in so many words, "Do a good job and the CEO position is yours." Since then he'd effectively managed the integration of Kentz and had been promoted to COO.

We did consider one other internal candidate and sent both of them to a four-day evaluation, which confirmed Neil was the right selection. It was probably the only easy decision we'd had to make in years.

Neil and Bob, while both highly skilled execs, could hardly have been more different in their styles. Bob was a deep thinker. My emails from him often ran hundreds of words long, meticulous in their detail. He talked in paradigms, and about vectors and forces and shifts that were happening in the energy and construction cycle. He could have been a very successful partner at one of the big strategy consulting firms like Bain or McKinsey.

Neil Bruce, on the other hand, had started in the engineering and construction business literally at the ground floor. He'd worked on a North Sea oil platform as a young man and rose up through the ranks over a thirty-year career in the construction and engineering business. His emails were usually no more than, "We need to do this, give me a call."

His board presentations were equally succinct. Instead of PowerPoint presentations we got quick summaries: "We're going to do this. Here are three reasons why. Any questions?"

Our board tradition—at least as long as I'd been there—was that after our committee meetings we'd go for dinner at the Mount Royal Club in Montreal. Sometimes only the CEO would join the board for the dinner, sometimes the entire senior management team would. After officially being named CEO in September 2015, Neil told me he no longer wanted to do dinners there.

"Why not?" I asked.

"It's too stuffy," he told me.

What Neil really meant was that he didn't want to wear a tie, as per the club dress code. In fact, the only time I ever saw him in a tie was in front of our shareholders at our annual general meeting or posing for his official portrait in our annual report. He was much more at home on job sites. When the two of us toured a hydro dam project on Vancouver Island, travelling there on a small float plane, the project managers and workers we met all loved Neil. He was one of them. He was able to size up a project quickly and to help the team deal with any problems.

Neil and Bob had one thing in common though. They shared a firm belief that the government of Canada ultimately wanted to resolve the charges against the company. Neil's experience in the UK—like Bob's in the US—taught him that government had no interest in destroying great national champions. Punishment was certain, but a DPA regime was the only logical outcome.

* * *

Bob Card had spent about a third of his time as CEO dealing with legacy issues—the corruption, the HR issues, the World Bank fallout, and the legal problems. When Neil stepped in, he had more time to devote to the job of actually running the company.

Nevertheless, a critically important element of his new role was convincing the powers that be that a DPA regime made sense, and not just for SNC-Lavalin. It served the national interest. Doing this while focusing on the core business was a tall order, a little bit like trying to replace the engine on a plane while it was in flight.

Journalist Yves Boisvert in the *Globe and Mail* said that "a DPA is not a way to get a crooked company off the hook: it is a way to make sure it is rehabilitated, watched and financially punished for what it did. All of that must be judicially approved and monitored. Should one of the long list of conditions be not respected, then criminal prosecution would continue, since it is only deferred as long as the terms are complied with. . . . Individuals involved in any scheme, too, are personally prosecuted in a Criminal Court. In other words, DPAs aren't soft on corruption—they're ways to ensure a company has cleaned up and pays the public for its misdeeds."

Our mission was trying to talk to anyone who would listen to us. Whether in the government, the opposition, the Prime Minister's Office or the Senate. If you were in Ottawa and you didn't know what a DPA was, you were soon going to find out.

The papers would later report that this lobbying effort included some eighty meetings. The clerk of the privy council, Michael Wernick, would describe it as the "most extensive government relations effort in modern times." In additional to lobbying government, we also set out to educate the business community about the value of a DPA law for Canada.

The media coverage often portrayed this as though it were a bad thing, involving some kind of nefarious, backroom dealing. This wasn't the case at all. We wanted everyone to know and hear what we were preaching. And while we were aggressive about spreading the word, our actual pitch began as more of a gentle prodding about the benefits of DPAs and why this legal regime was so important.

We encountered very little resistance. Virtually everyone we talked to seemed receptive to the idea that Canada should have a DPA law like the Americans and the British. And saw that it made sense why it would apply to SNC-Lavalin.

The stakes were still incredibly high. This was, after all, a life-or-death mission for the company. We assembled some well-connected help for this push. We asked anybody who knew anybody who could help us to spread the word —from former Prime Minister Jean Chrétien's aide Bruce Hartley to Prime Minister Brian Mulroney's longtime close adviser Bill Pristanski.

Mulroney himself emerged as an important ally, helping us in both Quebec and Ottawa. He saw value in both supporting an important Canadian company and of having a DPA regime in Canada. I was impressed by his willingness to put politics aside and put his weight behind something just because he thought it was the right thing to do. Canadians would get a glimpse of this when the former Conservative PM stepped up to help the Liberal government when then-US President Donald Trump decided to blow up NAFTA and renegotiate the free trade deal.

As chairperson I made the trip to Ottawa a handful of times to support the lobby effort. One was a cocktail party with various political staffers and members of Parliament, including Trudeau's Quebec lieutenant François-Philippe Champagne.

The most critical of these meetings was with Minister of Industry Navdeep Baines and five of his staffers. I was pretty blunt with Minister Baines when we met, telling him there's only three ways that this plays out: We go through a years-long legal process, and the company is found guilty, in which case we're dead. You have to close a Canadian company. Two, we go through the entire process, and SNC is found not guilty in the court of law. But even being charged puts the company in a horrible competitive position. Or there's the third option: we go the DPA route.

The first two options are very clearly bad, I told the minister. The government will have spent hundreds of millions of dollars and got nothing good in the end. If there really is no chance of cutting a deal, let's get moving with a DPA regime. What I had been taught in business school is that one should always understand what the best alternative to a negotiated agreement (BATNA) was. For the Canadian government, the BATNA were two dreadful outcomes and so a logical optimizing negotiator should have cut a deal. What this fails to recognize is that politics is about optimizing votes, and not economic outcomes.

Baines said all the right things in response. I wasn't expecting him to commit to anything. But he did seem to appreciate what we were saying: SNC-Lavalin is an important company that's trying to do the right thing. Along with Baines, we also seemed to find a sympathetic ear with the minister of finance, Bill Morneau.

Neil Bruce was also spreading the word at every opportunity. In January 2018 he was in Davos, Switzerland for the World Economic Forum Annual Meeting, where he met Morneau to brief him on the merits of DPAs and SNC-Lavalin's challenges. A month later he followed up with Morneau's director of policy in Ottawa to give him a document outlining in detail the reasons to support a DPA.

While SNC-Lavalin was leading this large lobbying effort for Canada's DPA regime—we were the company in the crosshairs, after all—we very quickly found widespread support, including from the Business Council of Canada, led by John Manley, a former finance minister and deputy prime minister.

I knew John from when we both sat on the board of CAE, the defence and aviation company best known for making flight simulators. DPAs had already been on the council's radar, so it was primed to join SNC-Lavalin's efforts. And it was a valuable partner, representing an all-star roster of executives and entrepreneurs.

Fear was a great motivator here. None of the companies on the council wanted to end up in the same spot as SNC-Lavalin. Not only did we face the risk of being wiped out. But all of our competitors were now using the charges against us as a weapon, telling prospective clients, "Why would you sign an eight-year contract with SNC to build something? They'll be out of business in a year."

But there were even bigger issues at play. For Canada to be the only major country that didn't have a DPA regime was clearly a competitive disadvantage. Operating in Canada, with its uncertain legal regime, brought companies additional legal risks.

In May 2015, Manley wrote an op-ed in the *Globe and Mail* pressing the legal case for DPAs.

"In Canada today," he said, "prosecutors have just three options if they believe a corporate executive or company has engaged in unlawful conduct. They can try to negotiate a guilty plea, go to court in hopes of securing a conviction or opt not to bring charges.

There's an obvious problem with this limited menu of choices. A guilty plea or a conviction can preclude a company from doing business with key customers in government, the private sector, and international organizations, in Canada and elsewhere. As a result, there is a strong disincentive for firms to report corruption or co-operate with the authorities.

Alternative enforcement mechanisms can be a much-needed addition to Canada's anti-corruption arsenal—a means of combatting corporate crime and punishing the guilty without hurting others who have done nothing wrong. They also can take into consideration the economic impact of the action taken."

The Business Council, along with Power Corp and SNC-Lavalin, funded a roundtable event to look at Canada's approach to white-collar crime in November 2015. Hosted by the Institute for Research on Public Policy, a Montreal-based think tank, a group of twenty-one people that included legal and academic experts gathered at a hotel in Toronto for the event. The consensus view that emerged, unsurprisingly, was that Canada should "seriously consider" adopting DPAs.

In 2016, the Business Council commissioned polling on public attitudes around DPAs. It found that there was nothing controversial about the subject. The public, like the business community, was actually very supportive. The Ipsos survey found that 87 percent of Canadians agreed that "it is unfair to innocent workers if unethical practices by a small number of people may jeopardize their jobs or the survival of the company."

Four-fifths of respondents said DPAs "can be a good way for companies to co-operate with authorities and make amends for wrongdoing without jeopardizing the jobs of innocent employees."

While SNC-Lavalin's government-relations team and our various allies orchestrated what was proving to be an effective campaign in Toronto and Ottawa, back in Montreal the struggle to outrun our past continued.

Yet another round of unhappy headlines appeared in October 2016 when Elections Canada said that SNC-Lavalin had violated the Elections Act, by illegally donating more than $117,000 to federal political parties between 2004 and 2011—the vast majority of it going to the Liberals.

In what was known as a straw-man donation strategy, employees and even their family members were instructed by senior executives to make donations for which they were then reimbursed by the company. The Charbonneau Commission had uncovered that this was widely practiced by engineering and construction firms in Quebec.

Our response was that this happened years before, and was, for all intents and purposes, carried out by a different company. The executives involved were all gone. But there was really no way to counter the deeply ingrained public view that SNC-Lavalin was deeply corrupt. Whatever we did seemed to be tainted by the past.

Perception was really the biggest barrier we faced. Why, people wondered, is Canada considering making a law (even if it is a good law that everyone likes) for the immediate benefit of one company? To many observers this just seemed inherently wrong.

There was also clearly a subset of people with a strong sense of justice who felt that no matter the facts, a DPA was letting a corrupt company off the hook. You don't let criminals get off with a fine, so why do we do that with a corporation? They want it to hurt. Of course, part of the problem with this line of thinking is that you can't put a corporation in prison, but never mind that.

"There is always going to be a segment of the population that will not be satisfied with any form of clemency or rehabilitation language. They want it to hurt. That's the point of it," explained Jennifer Quaid, a professor of civil law at the University of Ottawa, in an article about SNC-Lavalin in *The Walrus*.

Others saw in DPAs favoritism for big, politically connected corporations over small business. My response became well-rehearsed: the issue here is that three individuals were involved in a crime. How do you punish the corporation for what those three employees did? What is appropriate justice?

The United States ultimately learned why DPAs work the hard way, after it took down Arthur Andersen. This was the accounting firm involved in the 2001 Enron scandal, in which $100 billion in revenue was fraudulently reported. When Enron came under investigation, Arthur Anderson, the firm's auditor was accused of shredding documents and deleting emails to shield Enron.

Before the scandal, Arthur Anderson was a $4-billion company with 28,000 employees, one of the so-called Big Five accounting firms. Within months of being convicted of obstruction of justice, it was dead and gone—all to punish a few bad actors. It was a terrible outcome that very clearly no one wanted to repeat.

I was living in Paris at the time this happened, and one of the people I knew there, a fellow parent at the school my kids attended, was a partner at the firm. He was an American, so when Arthur Anderson collapsed, he was out of work and had to pack up his family and leave the country. It was unbelievably disruptive. This kind of pain inflicted on employees who had done nothing wrong would have played out in many thousands of homes.

By 2017, Canada's federal government seemed to be catching on too, launching public consultations on a possible DPA regime. In setting the stage for the consultations it stated: "The Government of Canada is considering the merits of implementing a DPA regime, not as a replacement for prosecution, but as an additional tool to be used by prosecutors. Since a company that complies with the terms of a DPA will avoid being convicted, the prospect of a DPA may encourage self-disclosure of misconduct, thereby enhancing detection and enforcement."

The consultations opened the door to a rigorous debate on DPAs: their advantages and disadvantages, what scope of offences they might cover, the conditions for negotiating one, how to monitor them and deal with noncompliance, and what international models a Canadian regime should follow. By this time Australia and France were about to join the UK and the US with DPA regimes of their own.

The consultations would involve forty meetings and gather forty-five submissions from interested parties, from businesses (including SNC-Lavalin) to NGOs. The early groundwork toward getting a bill was being laid.

8 | The third act

By early 2016 SNC's stock price had bottomed out at around $37 from a high of $61 at the start of 2011. The charges still hanging over the company and the endless uncertainty were taking a toll. The company was looking weak.

I left on a short trip for the Turks and Caicos for what I hoped would be a restful weekend getaway. Despite my best efforts to stay on as chair for only a year, I was well into my second year of working two jobs. I had hoped to hand the role over to one of the current directors, but when I consulted with the shareholders, they clearly wanted me to focus on finding someone not currently serving on the board who could take this on.

When the flight landed and I stepped off the plane into the warm Caribbean air, my phone immediately started chiming with missed calls and messages. They were all from Michael Sabia's assistant telling me to call him right away.

When I got Michael on the phone, he told me that SNC-Lavalin was in play. As head of the Caisse de dépôt et placement du Québec, our biggest shareholder, he'd been fielding calls from people who were thinking of taking a run at the company.

The depressed share price had made it a very attractive target for several foreign buyers. Because it had a strong balance sheet—over a $1 billion in cash or cash equivalents—and valuable assets like its seventeen percent stake in Ontario's Highway 407, any hunter could have effectively bought SNC-Lavalin and owned the core engineering and construction business for next to nothing. Essentially, the firm's market capitalization, given the depressed share price, meant that the non-engineering assets (such as Highway 407 and Altalink) plus the cash on the balance sheet would mean that any buyer would get the core engineering business for free.

The conversations going on revolved around one of the other big global engineering firms, working in conjunction with a hedge fund or financial buyer. The thinking was that they could snap us up and break the company in two with the financial buyer taking the non-engineering business and the engineering company the rest of it.

But potential bidders needed to find out if the Caisse would support a hostile bid. They understood the political stakes in taking over a Quebec icon.

Michael told me straight up that we should be very focused on keeping SNC-Lavalin independent and Canadian. Anxious to hear what else he knew; I quickly agreed and asked him what he was telling the callers. His answer to all of them, he said, was the same: They could take a run at SNC-Lavalin as long as they were willing to part with their first born.

I exhaled. It was a huge relief. Sabia could just as easily have entertained these offers. Most major pension funds would not have thought twice about it, and probably would willingly have sold to the highest bidder.

The Caisse wasn't biting because it was focused on long-term value creation, a rare position in Canada where there are no incentives for large pension funds to invest at home. At a time when many sovereign wealth funds are investing in their own countries to make them stronger, most of Canada's pension funds would rather invest outside Canada if that means getting a 0.1 percent higher internal rate of return. In recent years, Canadian pension funds have slashed their holdings of publicly traded Canadian companies. In 2023 it was just four percent, down from twenty-eight percent at the end of 2000. The eight largest pension funds in Canada now have more invested in China than they do at home.

The Quebec-based funds are the exception to this trend. The Caisse has a dual mandate. The primary focus is to maximize the return to its pensioners. But an important secondary objective is to ensure that it invests in Quebec to build strong Quebec companies that can compete globally. Building a toll road in Brazil might offer a great return, but it doesn't make Canada any better.

SNC-Lavalin's close call underscored an ongoing frustration of mine. Great Canadian companies have ceased to exist because owners, often with the government's acquiescence, have focused on short-term returns.

Take, for instance, Alcan. The 102-year-old aluminum maker, headquartered in Montreal, was taken over by London-based Rio Tinto in 2007 for $38 billion, sparking a debate about the hollowing out of corporate Canada. In the years before that, big names like Inco, Falconbridge, Dofasco (SP), Labatts, Molson and Hudson's Bay had all gone to foreign buyers. In the case of the Hudson's Bay the foreign buyer drove this iconic Canadian brand that had lasted centuries, into bankruptcy.

"The issue of whether there is so-called hollowing out in Canada is really an open question," said Finance Minister Jim Flaherty after the Alcan takeover. It seemed pretty clear, though, that Canada isn't well served when our industrial policy is hijacked by Wall Street hedge funds.

By all means, pension funds need to make maximizing returns their primary objective. But it's worth also making sure that there are strong businesses in Canada at the end of the day. The Canada Pension Plan Investment Board, the country's biggest pension fund, and others including Ontario Teachers, need to be looking out for the financial well-being of their pensioners forty or fifty years from now. That is the long-term liability that these funds must provide for. Investing to help develop Canadian champions today, even if it means forgoing a 0.1 percent return on investments is surely the right answer. Over the past ten years the assets of the top ten pension funds in Canada have increased by $1.2 trillion while their investments in Canada have remained the same in nominal terms and fallen 25 percent in real dollars. Given the current state of global protectionism one must ask whether this is smart policy. We need these investment funds to build pipelines, LNG plants and other critical infrastructure here in Canada.

It's no exaggeration to say that SNC-Lavalin only exists today in any form because at least one Canadian pension fund was concerned about the long-term financial health of the country. We had quietly dodged maybe the biggest bullet yet. It again underscored the urgency in getting our legal drama resolved. We just couldn't continue indefinitely in this state of legal limbo. We were very vulnerable in this period.

Imagine if the government's foot-dragging on the legal file had led to SNC-Lavalin's being taken over by a foreign buyer that would then have moved the head office out of Canada.

Fortunately, our game plan seemed to be paying off. By the end of the 2016 it was beginning to look like we just might make it across the finish line. We were hearing all the right signals from the Liberal government and from the Prime Minister's Office. There was overwhelming support in favour of a DPA.

The eight weeks of public consultations had attracted very little pushback. When the pros and cons of DPAs were weighed, there wasn't much to debate, aside from whether Canada should follow the US or the UK model. (The UK model seemed to be the favorite due to its narrower scope and closer involvement of the judiciary in the approval process.)

"The majority of participants (particularly those from the business sector)," read the government's final report, "thought that DPAs could be useful and cited advantages . . . but also mentioned the benefits of having a tool that avoided a binary (prosecute or not prosecute) outcome and that focused on rehabilitation rather than on punishment."

The report outlined the view that DPAs could ensure effective criminal sentences while also identifying more criminal activity through self-reporting, while also reducing the negative impact of convictions on innocent third parties, boosting compliance, and improving corporate culture.

Good news on the DPA front came in lock step with our rising business fortunes. Neil Bruce's business plan was beginning to pay big dividends.

In 2017 he came to me with an idea to buy W. S. Atkins, the UK-based engineering consultancy and project-management business. He thought it would be a perfect fit. Atkins was maybe half the size of SNC, with 18,000 employees, but the firm had an unbelievably strong public transport division. Mass transit projects are big and complex, and we were carving out a much sought-after expertise in the area.

Neil was also taken with its nuclear power plant decommissioning business, another growing market for SNC-Lavalin. On top of that, Atkins could strengthen our position in a number of key markets, including Europe and Saudi Arabia. The two of us headed off to London to meet with their CEO. We talked with him about the proposal over dinner, and then visited Atkins' current major project, the construction of a new underground route through central London, the state-of-the-art Elizabeth Line.

By spring, the $3.5-billion purchase was complete. As said, Atkins was a great fit, and there was one other benefit to the move: We had reduced our dependence on Canada, where Atkins did no business, and shifted our center of gravity toward London. It wasn't a driving reason for the deal but given that our Canadian business was at risk because of what the government was doing, it was prudent.

Importantly, investors loved the deal too. SNC-Lavalin's share price was once again the rise, quickly heading back towards its old highs.

Bruce had a level of ambition for the company reminiscent of Jacques Lamarre. His ultimate goal was to make SNC-Lavalin the top global engineering power. And by late 2017 this seemed like a realistic goal.

His play for Atkins marked a turning point. From a business perspective at least, the narrative began to shift. SNC-Lavalin looked impressive: It was growing (it now had 52,000 employees, up from thirty-five when Bruce started as CEO); it was well managed; and its legal issues sure seemed to be headed toward a resolution.

When I had first stepped in as chairperson, I made a point to go and meet with a sample of five of the top ten shareholders. These were generally big institutions or hedge funds. My intention was just to sit down and ask, "Hey, how you guys feel about the company?"

In my first go-round the answers were not all that encouraging. The responses now were night and day. The investors were impressed and optimistic. Business is great and the legal troubles are behind you, they'd say. I found myself having to temper their enthusiasm. "Actually, it isn't behind us *just* yet."

SNC-Lavalin was also continuing to change over its management. While Bruce had been building a new executive team, I was focused on refreshing the board. My mission was to have a board made up completely of new faces so that when the time came to talk to the government about a DPA, SNC-Lavalin could confidently go in with no ghosts from its troubled past.

Most of my fellow board members understood the logic and stepped down when asked. Only one resisted. What if stepping down implied that they were a part of the problem, tainted by the company's scandals? For me, though, this was non-negotiable. With some gentle arm twisting, the slate was cleaned. If you took a picture of the company's senior ranks and board in 2017 and compared it with photos from 2011, every face was different, save for mine.

We were, however, finally getting closer to resolving that, too. The subcommittee chaired by Jacques Bougie tasked with finding the next board chair had narrowed the list down to three possible people. Two of them were former high-profile CEOs with extensive governance experience. The other was Kevin Lynch, a former clerk of the privy council who had tremendous experience dealing with government.

Kevin was an economist with a PhD from McMaster University who'd started his career at the Bank of Canada and did a stint at the International Monetary Fund. He joined the public service and was deputy minister to Industry Minister John Manley from 1995 to 2000. He also served as deputy minister of finance. His big calling card, though, was his time as clerk between 2006 and 2009.

To anyone unfamiliar with the inner workings of the government of Canada, that might sound like an obscure job. In reality, it's one of the biggest. The clerk is the top job in the federal public service, overseeing hundreds of thousands of employees. It also encompasses the roles of secretary to the Cabinet and deputy minister to the prime minister. Kevin was clearly extraordinarily capable, and well versed in dealing with complex issues.

We took the list of candidates to a few of our biggest shareholders and asked for their thoughts. "Give us your pros and cons," we said. They wouldn't be picking the next chair, of course, but we also wanted to know if any names made them say "Over my dead body." All three names were well known and thought to be good candidates.

But Kevin's experience in Ottawa checked a box for us that no one else could. He had virtually built Canada's industrial policy under Manley; he had run the public service; and he served in senior roles under three different governments, Liberal and Conservative.

It seemed pretty clear to the search committee: If there's one person who truly understands how Ottawa works and how we can get this DPA passed and a deal done, it's Kevin. On top of that he was a deep thinker who understood foreign affairs and had a network in China. Creating joint ventures there to build Chinese nuclear reactors in other parts of the world was a promising business.

What he lacked, though, was senior corporate experience. To remedy this, we decided that we would bring him onto the board, but not as chairman just yet. He would spend some time working with me as vice-chairman, learning the ropes, before I finally made my exit from the board on December 19, 2017.

* * *

I had been on the SNC-Lavalin board for eighteen years. The last ones, enormously challenging and stressful. But I was lucky enough to be leaving feeling a sense of accomplishment.

I had lived through three distinct acts at SNC-Lavalin. The first, those early glory years from 2000 to 2011, when the company emerged as a financial powerhouse. The second, the tragic fall, where scandal exploded and from January 12, 2012, to September 12, 2012, share prices fell thirty-four percent. And the third act, redemption. The satisfying resurgence that saw shares rise sixty-one percent at a time when the TSX was up just thirty-seven percent. Our share price was now back up to the highs we had achieved before the scandal broke in late 2011. As I stepped off the board, with Kevin in my place, we seemed to be on a glide path to success.

SNC Lavalin was a very different company in 2017 than it had been in 2011. We had taken significant action and implemented new processes to make sure there would not be a repeat of what had happened in Libya. These changes included

- the appointment of a chief integrity officer who reported directly both to the board of directors and the general counsel of the company
- the complete renewal of the management team and the board of directors
- a mandatory annual code of contact conduct certification for employees, as well as additional targeted mandatory integrity training to ensure that there was complete understanding of the program

- a compliance investigation team that was separate from the internal audit function
- mandatory integrity checks for all third parties
- a supplier code of conduct
- the inclusion of integrity in the overall assessment of employees who were eligible for the annual incentive plan
- a reporting line operated by an independent service provider to report integrity concerns anonymously and confidentially
- the implementation of straightened policies and processes on topics such as anti-corruption and bribery, antitrust and competition, facilitation payments and conflicts of interests.

All of these initiatives we felt would position us for a deal with our government. We were winning big, high-profile projects such as the new Champlain bridge in Montreal and we had stabilized the senior team with several excellent additions, including Ian Edwards.

I was then, and I am still now, proud of SNC-Lavalin. It is one of Canada's great companies with a rich history, stretching back more than a century. The company has built some of the most important structures across Canada. From Hibernia in Newfoundland to the Canada Line in British Columbia, SNC-Lavalin engineers have built some of the most important infrastructure in this country.

That sense of pride in a business—something that's bigger than making money—can be a rare thing. I felt it at Chapters, watching young people reading in a store. I see it at Demers Ambulances, one of the companies I'm involved with through Clearspring Capital. When one of its ambulances rolls off the production line, the employees know it's going to be saving lives somewhere in the world, no matter where it ends up.

At SNC-Lavalin, I remember visiting the construction of the Canada Line in Vancouver with the board and listening to people who were so pleased with what the company had built. It played an important part in the success of the 2010 Vancouver Olympics.

One of my favourite memories of my time on the SNC-Lavalin board was when Jacques Lamarre took the entire board on a bus trip through Montreal. Every thirty seconds he would point to a structure the company had had a hand in building, from the Place des Arts to the Mercier bridge, to the Ville Marie Expressway, to so many others over the 2.5-hour tour. Even today, when I drive across the Champlain Bridge I find myself thinking, "Wow, SNC-Lavalin engineers built this." There are countless pieces of critical infrastructure like this that will be there long after we're gone. SNC-Lavalin built what matters.

In January 2018 my time as chairperson was up. I went out for dinner in Montreal with the senior management team, who I'd gotten to know very well. As a parting gift, knowing my passion for hockey and flying, they'd managed to get me four tickets to use Jeff Molson's box for a Canadiens' game, plus a four-day aerobatics flying course.

After a few glasses of wine, I gave a speech about how we were, thankfully, in great shape. All of us were feeling the warm glow of hope. We had changed both engines while the plane was flying! As I stepped off the board no single director remained who had served prior to the troubles. The same was true of the senior leadership team, the Office of the President. Looking at the top 120 executives in the company only seven had been in those positions back in 2011. This was a new team that finally had the wind at its back. And the feds were about to bring us welcome news.

Not long after, with the public consultations wrapped up, the Liberals announced in the federal budget on February 27, 2018, amendments to the criminal code to allow for DPAs, or as they would be called in Canada, "remediation agreements."

It might have been—*should* have been—a happy end to the SNC-Lavalin saga.

My father came to Canada from Scotland when he was 16 and taught himself to fly in this Fox Moth plane in the 1930s

As an experienced bush pilot when WWII began my father was sent to flight instructors' school and following three years instructing at St Hubert in Montreal he headed overseas to fly Mosquitos with the RCAF's 410 Squadron

My dad was my hero and we enjoyed fishing although I did not catch this one that was bigger than me. The best advice I got from my dad was to "do what's right even when no one is watching you"

I graduated from RMC in 1978 and the College instilled in me a great belief in its motto "Truth, Duty, Valour". I was honoured to escort the Queen as she left Ottawa in 1977 after celebrating her Silver Jubilee tour

In 1911 Arthur Surveyer (the S in SNC) opened a small engineering consulting firm on Saint-Francois-Xavier Street in Montreal. This was the seed that grew to become a global engineering giant, SNC-Lavalin

Manic-5, renamed the Daniel Johnson Dam, was one of SNC-Lavalin's signature large projects. Finished in 1968 in northern Quebec it was at the time the largest multi-arch dam in the world. SNC-Lavalin used their expertise in hydro-electric projects at home to win contracts for large dams around the world

SNC-Lavalin successfully expanded overseas with projects such as the Martyr's Arch in Algeria

SNC-Lavalin also had problem contracts such as the Goreway project which was a $757 million fixed-price contract for a gas-fired power project in Brampton, Ontario. The write-off caused by a supplier's bankruptcy led to a loss for SNC-Lavalin in the first quarter of 2007

A LIVELY HISTORY

IN 1990, AS SNC APPROACHED ITS 80TH ANNIVERSARY, LOCAL JOURNALIST SUZANNE LALANDE WAS HIRED TO WRITE A HISTORY OF THE COMPANY. *SNC: ENGINEERING BEYOND FRONTIERS* WAS COMPLETED NINE MONTHS LATER, AND PUBLISHED IN THE FALL OF 1991. PLEASED WITH HER WORK AND IMPRESSED BY HER BACKGROUND IN JOURNALISM, THE VICE-PRESIDENT OF PUBLIC AFFAIRS, ROBERT RACINE, OFFERED HER THE POSITION OF DIRECTOR OF PUBLIC AFFAIRS AND MEDIA RELATIONS.

nine regions. The new units would both provide the essential local element countries were demanding and give SNC-Lavalin an edge over the increasingly intense global competition.

The question remained, however: which countries and which sectors? Every division head seemed to have different answers. What the company needed was someone who could assemble all the various strategies into one cohesive plan for the international market.

Larry Stevenson and his colleagues at Bain & Company presented SNC-Lavalin's board with an analysis of its market share position across various sectors of expertise.

160 SNC-Lavalin: The First 100 Years

SNC-Lavalin published a history to celebrate the 100 year anniversary of the company. My introduction to the company had been a large strategy study that I led in 1990 when I was the Managing Director of Bain & Company Canada. The book highlighted that study as part of the history of the company

Jacques Lamarre hands over the reins to Pierre Duhaime in May 2009 as the new President & CEO of SNC Lavalin. The company had never looked stronger when Jacques retired

Fast forward two years and the bottom fell out as the SNC-Lavalin scandal was front page news for months and Pierre Duhaime was arrested for his role in the affair

On April 13, 2012 the RCMP raided SNC-Lavalin's head office in Montreal. The public perception was that the company was caught red-handed on this day. The reality is that the company had self-reported the scandal to the authorities two weeks earlier after our March Board meeting

The first indication of trouble was that Cynthia Vanier had been arrested in Mexico in November 2011. She was supposedly working on a project for SNC-Lavalin but in reality was working to get Saadi Gadaffi to Mexico. Although a pawn in the larger story Ms. Vanier may have suffered the most of all the protagonists as she spent 18 months in a Mexican jail

Left: On December 21, 1988 Pan Am Flight 103 blew up over Lockerbie, Scotland killing 259 passengers and crew and 11 people on the ground. I knew three colleagues on that flight. Right: They were sitting in business class and I visited the field a few years ago where the business class cabin came to rest

Many business associates ask me why we were in Libya in the first place as it was a terrorist state but they forget that Libya opened to the world when Tony Blair shook hands with Gadaffi in the desert. Our own Prime Minister, Paul Martin, seen here with the Libyan leader led a delegation of Canadian executives there to drum up business

The main culprit in the SNC-Lavalin affair was Executive Vice-President Riadh Ben Aissa seen here with Saadi Gadaffi, the son of the Libyan leader. Riadh was the Crown's key witness as they pursued SNC-Lavalin. Despite being the mastermind he never spent a day in a Canadian jail

I stepped in to be the Chairman of SNC-Lavalin in March 2015. Speaking at the company Annual General Meeting in Montreal

Me and Bob Card at the SNC-Lavalin AGM. Bob was our "Eagle Scout" and he took over a very troubled company. His focus was on getting the legal challenges behind us but his hope that this could be done in 2 or 3 years turned out to be way too optimistic

Bob Card handed over to Neil Bruce who had a deep engineering operating background. Seen here with me answering questions at the Annual General Meeting. Neil successfully lobbied for a DPA law in Canada but was then stunned when it was not applied to SNC-Lavalin

As SNC-Lavalin recovered it won critical high-profile projects such as the new Champlain Bridge in Montreal. The company ran an advertising campaign around the theme "Building what Matters"

Prime Minister Justin Trudeau hugging Jody Wilson-Raybould at her swearing in as Minister of Justice. The relationship would fracture over the SNC-Lavalin affair and threatened to bring down the Liberal Government

Gary Peters was the security man who claimed to be ex-SAS and who was involved in the plot with Cynthia Vanier to get Saadi Gadaffi to Mexico

Kathleen Roussel was Canada's Director of Public Prosecutions who was unwilling to negotiate a Deferred Prosecution Agreement (DPA) with SNC-Lavalin even though the government had just passed a bill authorizing DPAs with SNC-Lavalin specifically in mind

Canada's media and governments are generally anti-big business. This stance is perhaps good politics but bad policy. I faced that attitude when I ran Chapters as this Report on Business cover story illustrates. This was the headline despite the thousands of jobs we had created. The government held us up for nine months as we tried to compete online against Amazon. Today Amazon is the largest bookseller in Canada.

9 | A new ending

It started with a phone call. Government lawyers informed SNC-Lavalin on September 4, 2018, that the company was not going to be invited to negotiate a remediation agreement, or DPA. The charges against it were going ahead.

The same day, Kathleen Roussel, the director of public prosecutions, shared the news with the justice minister and attorney general, Jody Wilson-Raybould.

It's hard to underplay the level of shock and anger in the halls of SNC-Lavalin that day. It had been seven years of setbacks and struggles and effort to reform and resuscitate the company, and out of the blue, at the most unexpected point, it had been knocked back to square one.

Neil Bruce, who had always felt that SNC-Lavalin would get a DPA, couldn't believe it. He was livid.

This was all bad enough, but SNC-Lavalin was also told that not only would it not get a DPA, it would not even get a chance to make its case for a DPA.

The decision just did not make sense. The law had been brought in to level the playing field, to bring Canada in line with laws now in place in almost all the other industrial countries we competed against. And it had been urgently passed by the government *because* of the SNC-Lavalin case. The company was the prime example of why Canada needed this law. How could SNC-Lavalin not be invited to use a law that, for all intents and purposes, had been created *for* it?

The answer was that the decision rested entirely with Roussel, a long-time public servant who had been promoted to the top public prosecutor's job a year earlier, in 2017.

A lawyer who'd spent much of her career in Ottawa. Roussel had worked at Environment Canada and the Department of Justice. She grew up mainly in Hawkesbury, a small-town east of Ottawa. As a high schooler, she wanted to be a criminal lawyer, she told the *Globe and Mail* in an interview. Colleagues described her as "very focused on the law" and "unwavering in terms of her commitment to adhere to the letter of the law."

Bruce was angry but philosophical: "There's always disappointment in business and we'd deal with it", he thought. There was nothing official in writing, at least, which meant there might still be some wiggle room.

The senior executives at SNC-Lavalin frantically made calls, trying to get to the bottom of the decision and to see if there was anything the company could do to reason with the director of public prosecutions. Roussel's office agreed to receive more information. The company sent submissions in the form of lengthy letters to Roussel on September 7 and September 17, explaining why the company felt it had met all the necessary conditions to get an invitation to negotiate.

It also outlined to the Public Prosecution Service what could happen to the company without a DPA, including the dire scenario in which the company split apart and possibly sold off to a foreign rival. "We must humbly ask whether the public interest is served to prosecute SNC-Lavalin, and to try to achieve a guilty verdict. Such a decision would effectively lead to the end of SNC-Lavalin as we know it today and has been for more than 100 years."

The view inside the company was that these submissions were being flat-out ignored. SNC-Lavalin also tried legal avenues, filing for a judicial review of Roussel's decision. It was a long-shot and ultimately unsuccessful.

Weeks of working the phones got the company nowhere. On October 9, a final terse email arrived from Roussel's office: "An invitation to negotiate a remediation agreement is not appropriate in this case."

The company broke the news the next morning in a press release. Roussel had drawn blood, unfortunately most of it from Quebec pensioners who held many of the shares. By day's close, the share price had plunged fourteen percent, wiping out an astounding $600 million in shareholder value. This was not a loss suffered by some big anonymous hedge fund. Most of it represented the retirement savings of ordinary Canadians. These were the people who would be punished by the prosecutors' efforts to charge SNC-Lavalin.

On October 15, chairman Kevin Lynch called the Privy Council clerk, Michael Wernick, in Ottawa to say that he did not understand why the company was not being given a DPA. SNC-Lavalin had run into a brick wall.

Any decision to enter remediation negotiations is at the discretion of the director of public prosecutions, which seems reasonable enough. These are not meant to be political decisions. But what was maddening at this stage was that Roussel would not explain *why* she had made her decision. To those who knew the case, it seemed as if she was not working with all the facts, nor was she willing to listen to any outside advisers.

As the company's lawyers wrote in their application for a judicial review: "Far from providing compelling reasons to justify her decision, the DPP's letter gives no reasons to justify or support her conclusion that an invitation to negotiate was 'not appropriate'. She did not respond in any meaningful way to the voluminous information provided by the Applicants, and her reasoning cannot be discerned. The Applicants are in the dark as to how they failed to meet the requirement of 'appropriateness,' or why the public interest requirement, though met, has been ignored."

Even-handed journalists who had been reporting on the file were also taken aback by the news. "It is somewhat baffling," wrote the *Globe and Mail*'s Konrad Yakabuski, "that the director of public prosecutions chose to reject the company's application for such a deal and opted to subject SNC-Lavalin to a potentially endless criminal proceeding that could sound its death knell."

He added that "seeking to convict a company for crimes allegedly committed by one or a handful of employees has its downsides." Even if the company had been able to get a trial it would mean years of uncertainty and during this long period the company would have been regarded as "guilty until proven innocent."

Other high-profile figures joined the chorus. "If there was ever a case for a DPA," wrote Donald Johnston, a former attorney general and justice minister in *The Montreal Gazette*, "it was here. Canada had an opportunity to illustrate how corporate wrongdoing can be addressed effectively without destroying globally competitive companies, leaving jobs, skills and technologies to be profitably harvested abroad."

Roussel would eventually get around to explaining herself, not to the company but in a newspaper interview in 2020. There were, she would explain to the *Globe and Mail*'s Ottawa bureau chief Robert Fife, three main reasons why SNC-Lavalin didn't get the invite to negotiate.

First was the gravity of the corruption in Libya and elsewhere. "The factor that really weighed against a remediation agreement was really the 'severity and breadth' of the offence," she said. It was a "pretty unprecedented offence in Canada." She told the *Globe* this referred to both Libya and past incidents of corruption in other countries.

Second, the involvement of senior executives: "If you look at the hierarchy of the company, how high the scheme went . . ."

A third reason given was that the company did not self-report the crimes, a key condition for a DPA.

Let's look at each of these reasons in turn.

On the "severity and breadth" of the offence, it's true there had not been a case like this in Canada. (Canada didn't have a DPA regime, but never mind.) But there were many outside examples, like the Siemens case, in which companies had been offered DPAs. Literally hundreds of companies—even ones that did business inside Canada—had done far worse and had been granted DPAs. Why was all this precedence being ignored?

On her reference to "past incidents of corruption in other countries," I have to assume Roussel was referring to the Padma bridge project in Bangladesh, for which the World Bank imposed a ten-year ban on SNC-Lavalin. Under CEO Bob Card, the company agreed to the ban to clean house and to prove that corruption would not be tolerated in the new SNC-Lavalin. And it is important to note that the charges against the three junior SNC-Lavalin employees were thrown out by a court.

On the second point, Roussel is correct: this scheme in Libya involved a senior executive vice president and that executive vice president's finance officer. It also implicated the CEO. No one denies that these individuals did wrong. All of them were fired. Many more people were also pushed out of the company in the wake the crisis.

Virtually every transgression worldwide that has led to a DPA involved many of the senior executives in those companies, from the Siemen's case to BAE Systems to Airbus. The very reason that DPAs exist is so that those senior individuals can be prosecuted without harming innocent parties in those companies. How had Roussel so badly lost the plot on this?

SNC-Lavalin was a very different company now, too. Every single member of management and the board had been replaced. Why would someone want to destroy a company that had so eagerly embraced change and reform, from building a massive compliance department to welcoming a World Bank monitor into the fold—someone who went on to give it positive reviews?

"Just because," seemed to be Roussel's answer. As she explained to the *Globe*: "It is true SNC-Lavalin at the time I was dealing with them wasn't the company that had committed the offence, but once you put all the various factors together and weighed them, I came out on the side of a prosecution was still the way to go."

So instead of applauding the new management team for the reforms and changes they had made she was trying to punish people who were not even there when the events occurred.

The third explanation given was that SNC-Lavalin did not report the malfeasance. Vincent Larouche reported the DPP as saying, "because the enterprise did not report the malfeasance, we refused to give SNC access to a DPA." That was the most jaw-dropping of all because it was demonstrably wrong.

SNC-Lavalin *had* self-reported the same day it found out about the missing funds. I was in the boardroom when it happened. We had two different law firms at that meeting and the decision was made to alert the authorities immediately to the fact that sums of money were missing.

All of this happened on March 26, which was weeks before the RCMP raided the SNC-Lavalin head office on April 13. To this point in time, the company had *never* been contacted by the authorities.

It became a common misconception that the first contact between the company and the authorities was the high-profile RCMP raid. Even those who had been closely following the file got it wrong, and even long after the event. Writing on the case in the March 19, 2019, edition the *Globe and Mail* wrote "In SNC-Lavalin's case, the company does not appear to have disclosed information to police about alleged wrongdoing involving the former head of its international operations, Riadh Ben Aissa, before the RCMP conducted a raid on the company's Montreal head office in April, 2012."

The *Globe* wasn't the only outlet to repeat this error. In a column in *Maclean's* magazine, Tom Parkin explained that SNC-Lavalin did not get a DPA because it didn't alert investigators to the wrongdoing.

I can understand how casual observers following the headlines would have been led astray. Companies that get raided don't seem like companies that are cooperating. But how had Roussel, the ultimate insider, got such an important and obvious point so wrong?

The director of public prosecutions must have had an extremely narrow interpretation of self-reporting. Recall that the RCMP learned about the missing funds from Swiss investigators, not the company, because at this point the company didn't *know* about them. The police beat SNC-Lavalin to the reporting punch. Of course this raises the question: How could SNC-Lavalin have self-reported something it didn't know? The company did self-report everything it knew as soon as it knew it and opened its books to investigators.

I am struck when looking back at the coverage of this case that in Roussel's comments about the decision, she talks in the first person: "*I* didn't feel." "*I* came out on the side." This was not about her office or her team. It was one person's decision and view of the case. And, as the company would soon find, differing advice and opinions from some great legal minds were not welcome.

There was another unspoken reason why Roussel may have been eager to plow ahead with charges: overconfidence. The Crown's "star witness" was Riadh Ben Aissa. Ben Aissa had gained financially from his crimes, and been ordered to pay SNC-Lavalin back millions of dollars. Prosecutors were trying to charge SNC-Lavalin while working with the actual criminal.

Ben Aissa had obviously convinced Roussel that other executives and even the board were involved in his crimes. Yet his explanations and finger-pointing were ridiculous. At a preliminary hearing for Stéphane Roy, he said: "The company, the CEO, the office of the president, the board of directors were aware of Saadi Gaddafi's visits." Hell, of course we were—the board had been invited to a reception he attended in Montreal. What we *did not* know was that Ben Aissa was going to spend $1.8 million entertaining Saadi, including $30,000 for escorts.

He also testified in the Roy case, "These were contracts we got thanks to the influence, to the involvement of Saadi Gaddafi. I didn't do this on my own. The company pushed me to do it. I am a company man. I did what the company asked me to do. Yes, it was criminal. I pleaded guilty."

Certainly, we knew that the relationship that Ben Aissa had with Saadi was important to us winning business. That is often the case anywhere in the world. You win contracts by building strong relationships and the board encouraged him to win business in Libya. What the company and the board *did not* encourage Ben Aissa to do was to pay bribes to Saadi and to siphon off company money for his own accounts. The company Code of Ethics expressly forbid this.

All these details, though, underscored that this was a shaky case for the federal prosecutors. The big picture was no better. Canadian prosecutors were going in one direction, while the rest of the of the world was going in another. A case like this had never gone to trial in the US, for instance. It would have been settled with a DPA.

With zero global precedents, it was a risky path. But it was also a very risky and dangerous path for the company as it would effectively be "guilty until proven innocent." Business would be lost as a result.

Canada's western counterparts were going the extra mile to not destroy their national champions, even when they broke the law. Across all the biggest industries—from transportation to communications to aerospace to defence—the use of DPAs was being widely used to act quickly and decisively to make the needed changes and to make sure they protected the company and its employees, suppliers, and customers.

In some cases, even the self-reporting condition was put aside. In 2017, Rolls-Royce received a DPA in the UK, and agreed to pay £497 million to settle bribery charges spanning twenty-four years and at least seven countries. Rolls-Royce did not self-report but was credited for its "extraordinary cooperation." The case weighed the impact on innocent third parties and the company's remediation efforts but—importantly—didn't rule out the possibility of individuals' being prosecuted.

"People would tell me that Canada was out of step with the rest of the world," Neil Bruce recalled. "Senior US people would say that their objective was to punish individuals who do wrong and rehabilitate the company. 'But in Canada, you guys are doing the opposite.' Get the bad guys and don't harm the innocents should be the goal."

* * *

The Roussel decision had backed SNC-Lavalin into a corner. Along with the threat of its possible demise, it had to consider the immediate fallout. The company was building some of Canada's highest-profile infrastructure projects. Hiring the talent needed to deliver those projects on time and on budget suddenly got a lot tougher. The company was also likely to start losing worldwide contracts, and with them Canadian engineering jobs. SNC-Lavalin was once again at risk of being bought out. Inside the company, the pressure was on.

The firm switched gears yet again in its lobbying efforts. The plodding educational campaign that had won people over on the merits of DPAs became a full-court press to appeal Roussel's decision.

Neil Bruce wrote an open letter that appeared as a full-page ad in newspapers. "This situation could happen to any Canadian firm trying to seek settlement discussion," he wrote. "It is not just about the enormous impact on a Canadian company and all the innocent people dependent on it, including 9,000 Canadian employees, as well as Canadian pensioners, clients and investors. It is not just about numerous business partners, many of which are Canadian small business owners, who form the very backbone of the country's economy. It is not just about the 10,000 employees across Canada that, through no fault of their own, left our firm since 2012 due to the uncertainty, while our global employee base has doubled in size. This debate is about what is right for this country."

Bruce ended with an apology: "The truth is, the events prior to 2012 that led to the federal charges should never have taken place. The management team at SNC-Lavalin is entirely new and I apologize to all for the shortcomings during that period. In the years since, we have worked tirelessly to achieve excellence in governance and integrity because we want to regain the confidence of all our stakeholders and employees and mostly, that of all Canadians."

SNC-Lavalin, meanwhile, contacted officials in the Privy Council Office and the Department of Finance in search of advice on a path forward.

Up to this point Kevin Lynch had been perhaps overly cautious in his dealings with Ottawa. For all the obvious advantages of having the former privy council clerk on the board, there was a downside he had to deal with: the public perception that he had connections that could potentially be abused. I suspect this was hard on him. But the company needed him now.

SNC-Lavalin had also hired former Supreme Court Justice Frank Iacobucci as legal counsel. Originally, it wanted someone on the team who was above reproach to negotiate a DPA with the government when the time came. With the DPA off the table, he was pressed into other duties.

There were signs almost from the beginning that we were about to lose the PR war in this last battle. When the Liberals announced changes in the budget to allow for DPAs, a member of the party's own caucus immediately raised concerns. Member of Parliament Greg Fergus said DPAs could lead to white collar criminals getting a "slap on the wrist."

"It seems we're letting those with the means have an easier time of it than those who don't have the means."

Anyone who had paid any attention to the public consultations would have known that DPAs are not at all about skirting punishment. Again, there is no get-out-of-jail free card. But the message clearly hadn't reached the masses. Even the well-connected ones.

Maybe we were naive to think things would have moved ahead smoothly. At least one of my colleagues on the SNC-Lavalin board had predicted trouble. "I was hoping for a DPA for the company but frankly I was not surprised that a DPA was not offered and I thought it was not going to be offered for political reasons," said Jacques Bougie, a former CEO of Alcan and highly experienced board director.

The general view of SNC-Lavalin, as the sinister plotter, was captured in a *Walrus* magazine article written by Max Fawcett that appeared in August 2019: "The engineering giant was hardly shy about trying to get what it wanted," Fawcett wrote. "It helped fund a 2016 report, published by the Institute for Research in Public Policy, that made SNC Lavalin's case for a DPA, then it laid down covering fire in the form of full-page apologies in four major Canadian newspapers. There was even a video with Bruce, in October (2018), in which the CEO warned about the cost to the 'innocents' (such as employees, shareholders and pensioners) should his company be refused a DPA. These efforts felt more like a PR campaign than a show of genuine contrition."

Arguments like this conflated the early lobby efforts to get a DPA law in Canada with the period after the company learned it would not be getting one. Inaccurate and worse, this view of SNC-Lavalin struck me as unfair. What would critics have had SNC-Lavalin do at this point? Should it have thrown up its hands, laid off employees, and wound down the business? Gone looking for foreign buyers?

The magazine was right at least to say that SNC-Lavalin was not shy. It couldn't afford to be. Talking about the impact on innocent parties was often seen by critics as a bluff—part of SNC-Lavalin's hard sell to get its way. Some thought the company was using the threat of thousands of lost jobs in Quebec, a politically important part of the map for the Liberal Party, a gun to point at the government's head. It is worth pointing out that already at this stage thousands of high paying engineering jobs had been lost as a direct result of the company's time in the penalty box. As Neil Bruce had pointed out publicly, some 10,000 employees in Canada had left the firm since 2012 at a time when the rest of the company was doubling its employee base. Further delays made future additional job loses a very real and ongoing worry. A guilty charge meant no government contracts for a decade. The end of SNC-Lavalin, full stop. I was reminded of the oft-quoted lines from Ernest Hemingway's *The Sun Also Rises* when Bill asks, "How did you go bankrupt?" and Mike responds, "Gradually and then suddenly." SNC-Lavalin was facing the "suddenly."

In its efforts to get a DPA regime, the company met fourteen times with PMO staff, including Gerald Butts, principal secretary to the prime minister, and the PM's senior Quebec adviser, Mathieu Bouchard. But the focus and urgency of its efforts changed the day after the Roussel decision came down. The company fired off a research document to the PMO titled, SNC: "Thanks for Nothing, DPPSC (director of public prosecutions)." It outlined the dire scenario that could come with criminal prosecution. Similar communications followed in the coming weeks.

This hard sell was probably overkill. SNC-Lavalin quickly found it already had a solid supporter in the prime minister. Trudeau and his staff, it turned out, were just as puzzled as SNC-Lavalin by Roussel's decision.

Trudeau, according to the ethics commission investigation at which he later testified, thought that "SNC-Lavalin was precisely the kind of candidate for which the remediation agreement regime was designed: one that had taken significant steps to reform itself and whose conviction would harm many people who had not been involved in the wrong-doing. He recalled being concerned that the impact of the Director of Public Prosecutions' decision would extend beyond the case of SNC-Lavalin, and that it might be treated as a precedent for the decision to offer or not offer the opportunity to negotiate a remediation agreement in other cases."

He also testified that "a remediation agreement regime offered a way through for SNC-Lavalin, as had been the case for other large engineering firms in Europe, which had benefited from this type of regime."

But Trudeau's view wasn't necessarily the one that mattered most at this point. Jody Wilson-Raybould, minister of justice and attorney general, was standing firmly behind the director of public prosecutions.

Wilson-Raybould and Trudeau, two strong-willed politicians with very different agendas and an increasingly hostile relationship, were about to clash head on. And SNC-Lavalin was right in the middle.

10 | Enter the politicians

On November 4, 2015, together with thirty other new ministers (including the prime minister), Jody Wilson-Raybould was sworn in to Cabinet. It was an historic moment for the fresh-faced government of Justin Trudeau, who had personally recruited Wilson-Raybould. As Canada's first Indigenous justice minister in the first ever gender-balanced Cabinet, she was a powerful symbol of change.

At the swearing-in ceremony at Rideau Hall, the pair clasped each other shoulders, facing off almost nose-to-nose. A photo of this embrace came to define the optimism and "sunny ways" of the early days of the Liberal government.

Expectations on her could not have been higher and Wilson-Raybould instantly became one of the big stars of federal politics. She was from outside the Ottawa bubble and highly accomplished—a former Crown prosecutor, treaty commissioner, and regional chief of BC for the Assembly of First Nations. Her father was a hereditary chief who had sparred with Trudeau senior over Aboriginal rights in the Constitution. After her parents split when she was young, she was raised by her mother, a non-Indigenous teacher, on Vancouver Island, and credits her grandmother with teaching her culture and values. Following in her father's footsteps, Wilson-Rayboud had hopes that she could work to remake the relationship between Indigenous people and the Crown.

But in the political world where party loyalty and discipline matter above all else, Jody Wilson-Raybould was not necessarily the kind of teammate that Trudeau was expecting.

The relationship between the two of them was badly strained almost from the get-go. "A number of times over the first years of my government I grumbled to myself that it was difficult for me to not have a minister of justice that I was super-sympatico with," Trudeau told CBC journalist Aaron Wherry for his book *Promise and Peril: Justin Trudeau in Power*. "But it wasn't the kind of relationship that I would have ideally imagined, I don't think [it's what] she would have ideally imagined."

Wilson-Raybould's expectations and desire for big change—particularly around Indigenous reconciliation and criminal justice reform—seemed to crash against the reality of Ottawa policymaking and politics. "Wilson-Raybould did not have the experience of most of her predecessors in partisan politics and ended up having little patience for it, pushing back hard when staffers tried to discuss politics," wrote investigative journalist Stephen Maher in his book about Trudeau, *The Prince*.

She was also frustrated with Trudeau's insulated style of leadership and surprised that he didn't make himself directly accessible to Cabinet ministers. She said in her book *"Indian" in the Cabinet: Speaking Truth to Power*: "I believed I was being appointed because I had a different world view, because I had in-depth knowledge and experience. . . . I realized I was simply an Indian in the Cabinet."

In early 2018, Trudeau delivered a historic speech in the House of Commons on what his government was calling the Recognition and Implementation of Rights Framework. It was a game-changing legislative proposal that would put recognizing Indigenous rights front and center in all dealings with the Crown. It was the kind of transformative change Wilson-Raybould had come to Ottawa to fight for.

But it pretty quickly became obvious that nothing was going to happen soon. Some First Nations leaders were unhappy with how the file was being handled by Crown-Indigenous Relations Minister Carolyn Bennett. Wilson-Raybould was also unhappy with the approach and that change wasn't moving fast enough. She reportedly asked that she be allowed to take over the file—she had the expertise and experience to stickhandle it—but that was rejected.

As she would later write in the *Globe and Mail*, "Time and again my experience was symbolic inaction and ineffective baby steps were privileged over transformative efforts to address Canada's colonial legacy, systemic racism and the challenges with our criminal justice system. Too often, political expediency triumphed over bold and necessary action."

The promise to table the legislation by the end of the year was soon scrapped. The relationship between the PM and the justice minister, may not have reached a breaking point, but it seemed already doomed.

SNC-Lavalin dropped smack in the middle of this political breakdown and jurisdictional fight. In the months after Roussel's DPA decision, SNC-Lavalin was not the only party trying to get to the bottom of what had happened. The Prime Minister's Office and the Privy Council Office—the nerve center of the federal public service—were asking questions about why a DPA had been refused. Wilson-Raybould was on the receiving end.

Already angry with what she would later call Trudeau's broken promises, she seemed to view this file as one of those cases of politics getting in the way of meaningful work. She was quick to characterize questions from the PMO as efforts to bully her into reversing the decision.

Wilson-Raybould was in a unique position as both justice minister and attorney general. The first is a political job—a member of a team of elected Cabinet ministers. The other, the top legal officer of the land, is a position where political direction is not allowed. To Wilson-Raybould any reference to the SNC-Lavalin case struck her as crossing a line.

By February 7, 2019, the escalating back and forth between Wilson-Raybould and Trudeau over the SNC-Lavalin case dropped onto the front page of *The Globe* with devastating results for the government: "PM pressed Wilson-Raybould to abandon prosecution of SNC-Lavalin; Trudeau denies his office 'directed' her."

Everything changed the day the *Globe* story appeared. Up to this point, the SNC-Lavalin saga had largely been a business story. Politicians had been lobbied to pass a DPA regime, but nothing about that had been out of the ordinary or improper. All of it was out in the open and carefully documented. Then the SNC-Lavalin story suddenly became "the SNC-Lavalin scandal."

On one side, there was Trudeau and big powerful Quebec Inc, demanding the justice system bend to their will. On the other, the righteous attorney general, who sought to apply the law, according to her interpretation of this new law, no differently for any company, even if they're from Quebec or a friend of the prime minister's. Wilson-Raybould was the sympathetic —and to many, heroic—figure in this story.

To those of us who'd spent years working to fix SNC-Lavalin, going above and beyond to reform and save the company, the "SNC scandal" moniker seemed grossly unfair. This was a crisis entirely of the Liberal government's own making, an internecine war between the PM and his own justice minister that had been on a boil for some time.

In the weeks and months that followed that bombshell story, the scandal was put under the microscope by dozens of reporters, an ethics commission investigation, and a House of Commons justice committee. Taken altogether, their findings offer a pretty thorough account of what happened during a flurry of calls and meetings in Ottawa in the months after Roussel's no-DPA decision. A handful of these meetings and conversations became central to the drama of the fight between the PM and his Justice Minister.

On September 17, 2018, Trudeau and Wilson-Raybould met, at her request, along with Michael Wernick, the head of the public service, to discuss the case. Wilson-Raybould told the PM that after careful consideration, she would not interfere in the director of public prosecutions' decision not to offer SNC-Lavalin a remediation agreement.

According to Wilson-Raybould, Trudeau raised the upcoming provincial election in Quebec and the fact that he was an MP from Quebec as a concern, given what was at stake.

Trudeau later testified at the ethics commission review "that he had hoped that she would see that it was in the public interest to find a solution to the matter" but that "he knew throughout that it was Ms. Wilson-Raybould's decision to make."

"He said that Ms. Wilson-Raybould tended to view any form of engagement or advice by the Prime Minister's staff on decisions she had already made as 'interference.'"

Conversations were ongoing between staffers at the PMO, and the Justice and Finance Departments about what to do.

On September 19, Wilson-Raybould spoke with Finance Minister Bill Morneau outside the Commons Chamber on Parliament Hill. She told Morneau that his staff needed to stop contacting her office about the

SNC-Lavalin case and that "they were undermining the fundamental tenets of democracy and prosecutorial independence."

According to the ethics commission report, Morneau responded "by relaying the significant economic impact that could result from the Director of Public Prosecutions' decision to not pursue a remediation agreement with SNC-Lavalin and reiterated the appropriateness and importance of interdepartmental communications,"

In mid-October, SNC-Lavalin chairman Kevin Lynch called Wernick. Lynch was still frustrated that SNC had been left in the dark about the reasons for not being offered a remediation agreement and wanted advice. Wernick told him he had none to offer on a way forward.

By early December, Wilson-Raybould's patience was wearing thin. She met with Gerry Butts, Trudeau's principal secretary, for dinner at the Chateau Laurier and told him discussions about SNC-Lavalin needed to stop—she had made up her mind back in September and it wasn't going to change.

The two of them disagree about what happened next. Wilson-Raybould says that Butts said she needed to find a solution. Butts says that he only asked her to consider getting an independent opinion from someone like former Supreme Court Justice Beverly McLachlin about whether or not she could intervene.

The PMO had been eager for Wilson-Raybould to seek outside advice, in the hopes she would see that there were other valid opinions out there. "According to Mr. Trudeau, one of the sticking points was whether Ms. Wilson-Raybould was opposed, in principle and theoretically, to prosecution-specific directives," said the Conflict of Interest and Ethics Commissioner Mario Dion in the Trudeau II Report, "Having someone respected like Ms. McLachlin would help Ms. Wilson-Raybould understand that what she was being asked to do or what it was being suggested she do was not wrong for an Attorney General."

Things came to a head on December 19, when Wernick called Wilson-Raybould to talk. She decided to record the seventeen-minute-long call, anticipating that it would be "inappropriate."

Wernick started the call by saying that "our intelligence from various sources" suggested that SNC-Lavalin's board had been asking consulting firms about options for selling the company or moving it. "It seems to be real and not a bluff," he said.

(I was not privy to those SNC-Lavalin conversations, but almost certainly the board would have been considering the fallout of a criminal conviction and the possible takeover of the firm, which would see it leave Canada. As for SNC-Lavalin's deciding preemptively to exit the country, that was no longer an option given the conditions of the Caisse's investment in the company to help support the Atkins acquisition which precluded the option of leaving Canada.)

"The Prime Minister wants to be able to say that he has tried everything he can within the legitimate toolbox, so he is quite determined, quite firm, but he wants to know why the DPA route which Parliament provided for isn't being used," said Wernick. "I think he's going to find a way to get it done, one way or another. So, he's in that kind of a mood, and I want you to be aware of it."

The situation had never been put so bluntly. And coming from the head of the non-partisan public service, it carried an extra sting. When Raybould's staff released the recording to the public, it was another bombshell.

There is no denying that Wilson-Raybould was under pressure from her colleagues and her boss to review the decision. All of them had been expecting a certain, logical, outcome and had been caught off guard by Roussel's decision, which didn't add up. And all of them were worried about the economic fallout of killing SNC-Lavalin. The real question, though, is whether this pressure was improper.

Wilson-Raybould clearly felt any mention of the case amounted to political interference in her role as attorney general, a job which, she would write in a later memo, "must be non-partisan, more transparent in the principles that are the basis of decisions, and, in this respect, always willing to speak truth to power."

That was a great line that played well but it wasn't exactly what Jody Wilson-Raybould was doing. The dual role of attorney general and justice minister is guided by a convention known as the Shawcross Principle, named after the UK attorney general of the same name. University of Toronto law professor Kent Roach describes it as follows: "The Shawcross Principle is a constitutional convention that says the attorney general is entitled to consult with Cabinet colleagues about the policy implications of prosecutorial decisions, he or she is not to be directed or pressured on such decisions by the Cabinet." The principle lays out three important considerations:

- The attorney general must take into account matters of public interest
- Any assistance from Cabinet colleagues must be limited to advice
- The responsibility for the decision is that of the attorney general alone.

After examining the facts of the matter, Ethics Commissioner Mario Dion claimed that the prime minister breached this convention because, although he had not directed Wilson-Raybould to make the decision he wanted, he had pressured her. The Trudeau version of the event is very different. As Wernick explained in his testimony, "When you boil it all down, all we ever asked the attorney general to do was to consider a second opinion."

I tend to agree with Wernick because of the first bullet point above, which says that the attorney general "must" take into account matters of public interest. This, Wilson-Raybould did not do. The fact also stands that Trudeau did not override her decision.

Writing about this point in *Canadian Lawyer*, John Edmond, a retired member of the Law Societies of Ontario and British Columbia, said, "Prosecutorial discretion is not absolute; a prosecutor sitting in her office, making such a decision alone, without broad consultation about numbers of innocent people affected and the intensity of those effects, is failing in her duty to determine the appropriateness of an agreement."

"If no such consultation occurred, as it almost certainly did not, and if Trudeau and colleagues believed (as they did) that prosecution would have serious consequences to innocent parties, I suggest they would be entirely justified in raising the matter with the minister of justice."

It's worth noting that the Shawcross Principle was born in the UK, where the role of attorney general and the role of lord chancellor and secretary of state for justice are held by two different people. The attorney general is an independent, nonpartisan lawyer whose legal advice is binding on the government. In this capacity, the attorney general is in charge of administering the law. The minister of justice, on the other hand, is responsible for the justice portfolio, including developing policy and drafting legislation for this area. Thus, it was Wilson-Raybould's responsibility as minister of justice to consult with Cabinet colleagues and to get their input on the implementation of this very important, brand-new law. This she was unwilling to do. Perhaps it is time to consider separating the two roles in Canada, too.

What was frustrating to SNC-Lavalin was that Wilson-Raybould could have intervened in the case if she wanted to, at any point until a verdict was delivered. Such an intervention, while an extraordinary step, is laid out in the Director of Public Prosecution Act. Her refusal wasn't really speaking truth to power; it was entirely within her power to act.

Wilson-Raybould characterized all questions about the case as politically motivated because they raised the very real negative repercussions of the decision. This took on a sinister tone—politicians putting fears about jobs ahead of "justice"—but it wasn't an unreasonable concern at all.

The public interest argument for settling the SNC-Lavalin case was obvious. SNC-Lavalin was in line for a DPA because no one, least of all the government of the day, wanted to see a leading Canadian company picked off by an American or European competitor and thousands of jobs go with it because of the work of a handful of bad employees. Any British, American, or French head of government would have done the same as Trudeau.

And yet throughout the scandal, Wilson-Raybould was celebrated for pushing aside these concerns. She wrote in her memoir that "during the SNC-Lavalin affair, there were clear attempts to bend the rule of law. But in this case, it was being bent towards injustice. Towards politically self-interested ends. Towards narrow and petty preoccupations that do none of us a service."

Language like that played well in the good vs. evil narrative that had taken shape. But I was shocked to see a senior Cabinet minister call the fate of a company and thousands of jobs "narrow and petty preoccupations." Wilson-Raybould obviously had important and worthy issues that were very important to her. Protecting jobs and helping Canadian businesses compete internationally were just not on the list.

Compare Wilson-Raybould's view to Morneau's, who wrote in his memoir, "Canada had adopted the remediation agreement regime in part because most of our allies had similar remedies, and we had a gap in our criminal law when it came to corporate wrongdoing. Prime Minister Trudeau favoured this approach, as did I, on the basis that would punish the firm while avoiding the loss of thousands of jobs."

"This would have been an entirely appropriate remedy for [Wilson-Raybould] to agree to or at least consider under the relevant statute," he added. "It would also save the viability of one of Canada's few truly global corporate champions, an outcome that I thought made a lot of sense."

Wilson-Raybould at some point must have understood this, too. She was the justice minister, after all, who had helped make DPAs the law of the land. And she did this with the belief that they applied to SNC-Lavalin. As she said in her call with Wernick, "From day one when people were talking about why we are entering into a or putting a DPA regime in place . . . Everybody knows it was because of SNC."

As weeks of tense and increasingly acrimonious argument made clear, however, there was no reconciling these opposing views. This was not, however, a case of two immoveable objects. On January 7, Trudeau informed Wilson-Raybould that she was being removed from the justice portfolio. A month later, she resigned from Cabinet.

As her final act as justice minister, in the few days between learning about the shuffle and leaving the post, Wilson-Raybould issued the Directive on Civil Litigation Involving Indigenous Peoples. It was a significant order, directing Crown lawyers to end Canada's "adversarial" approach to dealing with Indigenous parties. It encouraged settlements instead of protracted legal fights in front of judges. "Moving forward with recognition and reconciliation means we cannot continue to rely on adversarial court proceedings to lead the way," said Wilson-Raybould in a press release.

A column in the *Ottawa Citizen* described it as "the thunderclap at the stormy end of Wilson-Rayould's tenure as justice minister and attorney general. And given the timing, one wonders if it wasn't also a parting shot quickly discharged before her time as attorney general ran out." It was, no doubt, an important recognition of Indigenous rights. But some observers couldn't help but note at least a hint of similarity between this approach and remediation agreements.

Trudeau had got his way in the end, but at huge cost. He obfuscated and confused events by claiming he had never put pressure on his justice minister. He was caught off guard on an issue that should have been settled before it began.

I'm quite sure that if Trudeau had enjoyed even a remotely amicable relationship with his justice minister, all of this could have been avoided. Given the reality of their relationship, the Prime Minister would have been wise to shuffle Wilson-Raybould to another portfolio long before the SNC-Lavalin affair. It is hard to understand why he didn't. One ministerial staffer told Maher that the PMO contemplated moving Wilson-Raybould out of justice during "every single Cabinet shuffle from the time she was appointed until it actually happened." Trudeau could have had a justice minister in place who supported his, and his government's, intentions and policies.

The blowback led to Butts's resignation. In his resignation letter, posted on Twitter by the prime minister, Butts wrote: "I categorically deny the accusation that I or anyone else in [the PMO] pressured Ms. Wilson-Raybould. We honoured the unique role of the attorney general. At all times, I and those around me acted with integrity and a singular focus on the best interests of all Canadians."

Wilson-Raybould's departure was followed by one of Trudeau's most competent ministers, Jane Philpott, who resigned from Cabinet on March 4, 2019. Trudeau's Cabinet seemed to be crumbling, and heading into an election, it was unclear if he could recover from the debacle. Speculation swirled as to whether other Cabinet ministers would join the defectors.

After his unfortunate turn in the spotlight, Michael Wernick also announced his resignation. He had been dragged before a justice committee hearing to explain his role in the affair, which had sparked opposition doubts about his non-partisanship.

The Liberals had torn themselves apart and hurt others in their orbit over their own legislation.

Canada now had a new justice minister who was on the same side as the PM, but it was cold comfort for SNC-Lavalin. Public opinion was set in concrete: SNC-Lavalin was a villain, its name now forever linked to political scandal. Any goodwill that it had earned through building its compliance department, accepting the World Bank's punishment and monitor, and replacing its leadership seemed to evaporate.

* * *

That spring, in May 2019, a Quebec judge ruled that there was enough evidence for the SNC-Lavalin case to go to trial on charges of fraud and corruption. The company had expected as much. There was little more to do now on the legal front but prepare its defense.

A month later the company announced that Neil Bruce was retiring. He had sold his Montreal home and was planning to return home to the UK.

It was a tough end to his tenure. He'd done incredible work to build the business up again. He had hoped to hand over a company without the sword of Damocles hanging over the new CEO. But it was impossible to counter the government's efforts to bring SNC-Lavalin down. His goal of making SNC-Lavalin the world's biggest engineering firm were now a far-off memory. In the twelve months before his exit, SNC-Lavalin's stock price had plummeted sixty-one percent. And Bruce estimated that the legal saga had cost the company as much as $6 billion in new contracts.

After eight years under a cloud, SNC-Lavalin now had to actually prepare for its end. The board and new interim CEO Ian Edwards were working on a plan that would, the company said, "de-risk and simplifies" the business. Analysts speculated this could involve breaking the company up or killing off units like the once-dominant infrastructure division. There were only so many outcomes left.

11 | True crime

By mid-2019, SNC-Lavalin was in its darkest days, worn down by the events in Ottawa, its future uncertain. I spoke on occasion with Ian Edwards and had a coffee with Kevin Lynch to commiserate over what had happened. But I was a bystander now, watching like everyone else, the wreckage at the side of the road, flabbergasted at what had gone wrong. I thought we were on the five-yard line when I handed over the chairmanship. I had really thought we were in great shape.

SNC-Lavalin deserved to be punished, there is no doubt about it. But with the scandal in Ottawa and the trial looming, perspective seemed to have gone out the window. Worst of all, it seemed that the actual wrong doers were going to largely escape scrutiny and justice.

In the world of corporate malfeasance, this was an increasingly common outcome.

In 2003, after my time running Chapters, I became the CEO of Pep Boys, the big US automotive service chain. The company was struggling; it hadn't grown much in the previous two years and was facing stiff competition. The chain needed some new ideas and retail innovation.

The auto service industry is notorious for shady dealings, upselling customers on work their vehicles don't actually need. Faced with the pressure to boost profits and hit targets, it's easy to see why it happens.

When I arrived at Pep Boys, I told my direct reports that I was okay getting fired for incompetence. But I never want us to be charged with doing something illegal or unethical. There are lines that must never be crossed. Our solution at Pep Boys was to tie service manager bonuses to customer surveys, disincentivizing doing unnecessary work.

In the business world, there are far too many cases of executives at some of the biggest, most successful companies in the world who have crossed lines. And there were plenty of high-profile cases unfolding around the time of the SNC-Lavalin scandal. Many were ending with massive fines, a relatively new phenomenon in the corporate world.

A handful of these cases struck me as particularly egregious, and they provide useful context for understanding the SNC-Lavalin case and the handling of white-collar crime. These crimes were an order of magnitude worse than bribery. And, unlike at SNC-Lavalin, where the malfeasance was carried out secretly by a small group of people, these crimes were part of a corporate strategy. Yet these cases had similarly unsatisfying and unjust outcomes.

At the top of the list is Boeing.

On March 10, 2019, at 8:38 a.m. Ethiopian Airlines flight 307 took off from the Ethiopian capital of Addis Ababa on route to Nairobi, Kenya. Among those on the plane were three generations of a Canadian family from Brampton, Ont.: Manant Vaidya and his parents, Pannagesh and Hansini Vaidya, his sister and brother-in-law, Kosha Vaidya and Prerit Dixit, and their kids, Ashka and Anoushka Dixit.

Captain Yared Getachew was the pilot of the Boeing 737 Max aircraft. He'd flown more than 8,000 hours, including some 1,400 hours on Boeing 737s. The weather was clear, the pilots would report: CAVU (ceiling and visibility unlimited), a perfect day for flying. But a minute and fifty-five seconds after takeoff the pilots were having control problems.

Unknown to the pilots they were being overridden by a flight stabilizing feature developed by Boeing for the 737 Max aircraft. This feature, known as MCAS, or maneuvering characteristics augmentation system, is designed to push the aircraft's nose down automatically if the angle of attack is too large. In other words, if MCAS thinks the plane's nose is too high, it will, on its own, push the nose down and put the plane in a dive. This is exactly what MCAS did to Flight 307. The pilots battled to keep the plane airborne, but a little under six minutes after takeoff, Flight 307 cratered into a field sixty-five miles from Addis Ababa at 700 mph, killing all 157 people aboard.

The crash was eerily similar to another, only five months before. Lion Air Flight 610 was another Boeing 737 Max, headed from Jakarta to the island of Sumatra, Indonesia. This plane also had control problems shortly after takeoff, driven by MCAS. In this case thirteen minutes after takeoff the plane plunged into the Java Sea killing all 189 passengers and crew. The final accident report highlighted that flight 610 crashed because of aircraft design flaws and inadequate training.

The inadequate training was driven by the fact that MCAS was underplayed by Boeing. The company wanted pilots and airlines to believe that the 737 Max flew just like its predecessor, the best-selling earlier version 737s and thus required little pilot retraining which is very costly for airlines.

Boeing was for many years the dominant manufacturer of commercial aircraft. Some 10,000 planes were in the air in over 150 countries. Many pilots parroted the familiar famous refrain "if it ain't Boeing, I ain't going." The tide for Boeing turned due to two forces: one internal and the other external.

The internal force was the merger of Boeing and McDonnell Douglas in 1997. Shortly after the merger the CEO of McDonnell Douglas, Harry Stonecipher, stepped up to become CEO of Boeing. The Boeing culture was all about engineering excellence, but Stonecipher and the McDonnell Douglas senior executives were financial wizards. At one press conference Stonecipher responded to a question about the perception that he was only interested in making money. His response was, "you're right. I am." The bean counters now ruled.

The second force was the emergence of new competitors. Foremost amongst them was Airbus, which had been formed by a consortium of European aerospace firms. Airbus's first aircraft, the A300, entered service in 1974. Airbus successfully launched new innovative products, including fly-by-wire technology. By the turn of the century, Boeing and Airbus competed neck-and-neck.

Another competitor, the Canadian firm Bombardier, also was a factor in the 737 Max story. Bombardier launched a new aircraft, the C Series, which would compete with some of Airbus' and Boeing's best-selling smaller aircraft, including the 737. The C Series was fuel efficient and, when launched in 2013, was challenging the money-making sector for the Boeing/Airbus duopoly. Both companies had to react. Airbus launched the A320neo, which stood for New Engine Option. It was

15 percent more fuel efficient than the current aircraft it was replacing and was an instant bestseller.

Boeing opted for a quick solution rather than trying to design an entirely new aircraft. It launched the 737 Max with new fuel-efficient engines to match the offerings of its rivals. The challenge for Boeing was that the 737 is very low to the ground and so to make the new improved engines fit they had to move the engines farther forward on the wings. This caused a potential flight problem as engineers observed a tendency for the plane's nose to pitch up during certain maneuvers. A software solution was found so that the new 737 Max would fly just like the previous 737. It could save $1,000,000 per aircraft sold in pilot training and simulator costs. Mark Forkner, Boeing 737's chief technical pilot said in a March 2017 e-mail, "I want to stress the importance of holding firm that this will not require any type of simulator training."

Conversion to the 737 Max would be done by pilots on an iPad. This shortcut, which was approved by the FAA, would have dire consequences. Pilots, including the ones flying Ethiopian Airlines Flight 307 and Lion Air Flight 610, were often not aware of MCAS or how to deal with any malfunctions of the system. Training was essential as pilots needed to respond within ten seconds if there was an MCAS malfunction, otherwise the situation was not recoverable. And yet Boeing did not provide the needed training, nor did it even mention MCAS in the pilot manuals. The ownership of this fiasco went right to the top of the pyramid at Boeing.

Ed Pierson, the senior manager at the 737 Max factory, sent an e-mail to the head of the 737 program in June 2018 saying, "For the first time in my life, I'm sorry to say that I'm hesitant about putting my family on a Boeing airplane".

Not only did the 737 Max fly very differently than the prior 737s, but Boeing made it vulnerable by offering the plane with only one angle of attack sensor. This is the sensor that tells MCAS whether the nose is up or down. Most aircraft never have a critical component that can be a single point of failure. Airlines could buy a second angle of attack sensor to solve this problem, but this would cost them more and both Lion Air and Ethiopian Airlines had only one such sensor. Again, the bean counters at Boeing had prevailed over the safety culture.

So, all these problems were known well before the Lion Air crash. Yet Boeing did not ground all 737 Max to fix the MCAS problem. The company blamed the pilots despite knowing all the internal issues. Then a few months later came the second crash. Once again Boeing did not ground the fleet. In fact, it fought the FAA to keep the plane in the air. Only after most countries had grounded the 737 Max did Boeing accept the inevitable and ground the flawed plane.

So, what were the consequences for Boeing? Nothing until many months later after CEO Dennis Muilenburg had a disastrous session with Congress when he testified in October 2019. Two months later he left Boeing with a $6.2 million package. The board remained firmly in place. It had apparently been fine with the CEO allowing an unsafe plane to fly, fine with him not grounding the plane after the first crash, or the second crash, but they were not fine with his public relations mess up.

Boeing reached a deferred prosecution agreement with the Department of Justice and paid $2.5 billion in penalties. The 737 Max fleet was grounded for twenty months and by March 2020 the 737 Max file had cost Boeing a stunning $18.6 billion. Its troubles and safety issues continued, however. In 2024 a door blew off a 737 Max mid-flight. A few months later, the Department of Justice told Boeing it had breached the terms of its DPA protecting it from criminal prosecution. (Remember, the DPA is not a get-out-jail free card.)

The families of those killed in the crash wrote to Justice officials asking that the company and executives, including Mullenberg, face criminal prosecutions for the "deadliest corporate crime in US history." On May 23rd, 2025 The US Department of Justice announced a deal that would allow Boeing to avoid prosecution for the two fatal crashes. Victims' families were not happy but this avoided a trial that would have severely hurt Boeing's reputation and avoided Boeing being labeled a corporate felon which would have jeopardized many lucrative future contracts with the US government.

* * *

In the fall of 2019 Purdue Pharma was facing 2,900 lawsuits when it filed for bankruptcy restructuring, hitting pause on the claims. Purdue was the maker of OxyContin, the powerfully addictive painkiller. The opioid crisis this drug fueled has affected millions of people across the U.S. and Canada. It has claimed hundreds of thousands of lives and created a public health crisis of monumental proportions.

It has been especially lethal for our military veterans. In the US, overdose mortality rates for veterans increased 53 percent from 2010 to 2019 according to research supported by grants from the National Institute on Drug Abuse. Having served in the Canadian Forces for thirteen years I am particularly saddened when I read about the suffering that many of our veterans endure.

Kory Baker died of an overdose at age thirty-three on February 21, 2016. He grew up in Rochester and was a dean's list student in college before joining the US Army as a medic. He served in Iraq and after returning to the US suffered from post-traumatic stress disorder. To battle his PTSD, he started with OxyContin, which led to heroin. "If you're using pain meds like OxyContin, please know that they are incredibly dangerous, and can easily lead to heroin," wrote his parents in his obituary. "If you're a parent/sibling/friend, and you suspect someone is in trouble, it is probably much worse than you can imagine."

As brilliantly articulated by Patrick Radden Keefe in *Empire of Pain*, the Purdue story began in Brooklyn in 1920 when a trio of brothers, the Sacklers, made a family fortune by inventing the field of medical advertising as they aggressively marketed the sedatives Librium and Valium to doctors. Fast forward to the next generation, led by Richard Sackler, son of one of the founders, and the aggressive advertising mushroomed as the company sold billions of opioids.

The Sackler strategy was built around misleading advertising. They marketed OxyContin as weaker than morphine when in fact it was twice as strong. The active ingredient in OxyContin is oxycodone, which is a chemical cousin of heroin and two times more powerful than morphine. They claimed that less than 1 percent of patients would become addicted when they knew there was already widespread addiction. Interestingly, their advertising targeted general practitioners rather than pain experts, who knew about the addictive nature of opioids. Doctors were given all-expense-paid trips and paid handsomely to give speeches to marvel at the effectiveness and non-addictiveness of opioids.

In 2003, the DEA found that Purdue's aggressive methods had "very much exacerbated OxyContin's widespread abuse." In May 2007, Purdue plead guilty to misleading the public about OxyContin's risk of addiction and agreed to pay $600 million. Three senior executives were sentenced to 400 hours of community service. The prosecutors had recommended felony charges that could have sent top Purdue executives to prison if they were convicted.

The band played on as Purdue continued to make a fortune selling addictive opioids. It hired global consulting firm McKinsey to see if it could actually increase sales. As Nicholas Kristof points out in *Tightrope*, "McKinsey & Company advised Purdue on how to 'turbocharge' sales of opioids, how to resist drug enforcement agents and how to counter the emotional messages from mothers with teenagers that had overdosed." As reported in the *New York Times* on November 27, 2020, McKinsey advised Purdue Pharma to offer rebates to distributors whenever a patient overdosed on OxyContin. Basically, an incentive for overdoses.

Purdue paid McKinsey some $83.7 million in fees from 2004 to 2019 for this brilliant marketing advice. McKinsey then tried to hide the evidence. As reported in the *New York Times*, the leader of McKinsey's North American pharmaceutical practice wrote to another senior partner: "It probably makes sense to have a quick conversation with the risk committee to see if we should be doing anything 'other than' eliminating all our documents and emails. Suspect not but as things get tougher there someone might turn to us."

McKinsey eventually offered an apology and paid $600 million. Why did it risk a reputation built over generations? As former *New York Times* columnist Anand Giridharadas wrote, "[McKinsey] knew what was going on. And they found a way to look past it, through it, around it, so as to answer the only question they cared about: how to make the client money." And, I would add, how to make itself money.

McKinsey may have made millions, but the Sacklers made billions. The *Wall Street Journal* estimates that the Sacklers received at least $12 to 13 billion in profits from Purdue Pharma.

Not long after filing for bankruptcy, Purdue Pharma plead guilty to assorted federal charges. The settlement, valued at some $10 billion, included provisions for the Sacklers to pay $3 billion in damages and relinquish control of Purdue Pharma. As Keefe observes in *Empire of Pain*, no Sacklers and no executives were obliged to acknowledge guilt personally. It was "as if the corporation had acted autonomously, like a driverless car."

The Sackler name is now toxic. Opioids have killed more Americans than WWI and WWII combined and yet there have not been serious consequences for the protagonists in this tragedy. And none of the Sacklers or Purdue executives have spent a day in jail.

* * *

On August 25, 2017, Category Four Hurricane Harvey pummeled the city of Houston. Forty-eight-year-old Jill Renick was the director of spa services at the Omni Houston hotel and was trapped during the storm in an elevator that was rapidly filling with flood water. At 5:40 a.m., she called the hotel front desk and then called 911. Video would show later that Jill was able to pry open the elevator doors but then was trapped in the flooded basement. Her body was found eleven days later.

Hurricane Harvey killed eighty-seven other people. Over a third of Houston was underwater. The storm caused $125 billion in damage (second only to the 2005 Hurricane Katrina). Studies of Hurricane Harvey estimated that the rainfall was 38 percent higher because of climate change.

Climate deniers will say dangerous hurricanes have always existed. But the facts are the number of extreme weather events causing at least a billion dollars in economic losses has increased 400 percent since the 1980s. The dramatic increase in massive forest fires, floods, droughts, hurricanes and heat waves resulting from climate change are costing lives and significant economic losses. According to the Intergovernmental Panel on Climate Change (IPCC) the cost of climate change could be in the range of 1.6 to 5 percent of global GDP per year by 2050. The Global Commission on the economy and Climate estimates that the cost of inaction on climate change could be as high as $44 trillion by 2060.

In light of these almost unfathomable outcomes, one company's corporate malfeasance stands out. Volkswagen is one of the two largest automobile manufacturers in the world. It had long been a market leader in Europe but struggled in the US market, except for the brief love affair with the VW Beetle. Executives believed that the strategy to conquer the US was with diesel. Diesel had not done well in the US yet represented 50 to 60 percent of the market in Germany and France. VW paid $730,000 for a study in the US to demonstrate that diesel was more environmentally friendly than gasoline. The company ran ads and sold very well in North America. It saw a six-fold increase in the sales of diesel cars. VW and Audi (owned by VW) won prestigious Green Car of the Year awards in 2009 and 2010.

But it was all a trick. Vehicles are subject to extensive testing in the US before they can be sold to the public. VW's diesel cars all passed inspection, but only because of software designed to hide emissions like poisonous nitrogen oxides during testing. The so-called "defect devices" turned off when cars were being driven on the road. That led to better mileage and better vehicle performance but with very high emissions, which had not been detected by the regulators in test centres.

Executives believed that they would not be caught because it is very hard to test for emissions when a car is actually driving on the road. They did not count on the ingenuity of Dan Carder and some of his West Virginia University students. They were able to measure emissions coming out of the tailpipe while VW cars were being driven and they found that the NOx levels on the road-driven cars were 40 to 80 times higher than in lab results. Devices had been put on over 11 million vehicles worldwide for the model years 2009 to 2015 to fool regulators and the public.

VW executives would first try to cover it all up and then cowardly tried to blame these devices on three lower-level executives. As Jack Ewing wrote in the *New York Times,* the truth was that "higher ups overruled engineers who objected to the illegal software." In fact, it was an open secret in Germany. Hundreds of executives were involved in this cheating scheme.

VW CEO Martin Winterkorn was forced to resign in September 2015, a week after the scandal broke. He claimed he was not aware of the devices but was indicted in the US in May 2018 on charges of fraud and conspiracy. The SEC argued that Winterkorn and other VW executives were made aware of the defect devices as early as November 2007. Germany charged Winterkorn shortly after, in April 2019.

It wasn't until 2021 that the company announced it would seek compensation from its former CEO, who agreed to pay VW about $14 million for "breaches of due diligence."

Given VW's prominence in Germany it is not clear that the German authorities would have pursued this case were it not for the detective work at West Virginia University and the US regulatory authorities. As Ewing summarized in the *New York Times*, VW executives "concocted an elaborate cover up when regulators became suspicious and . . . destroyed evidence once they realized they would be exposed."

Two employees out of hundreds who likely knew about the cover-up were given prison time in the US. One US-based executive was sentenced to seven years in prison and fined $400,000 in 2017. The other, an engineer, was sentenced to forty months in prison and fined $200,000 for his role in what the judge in his case called a "stunning fraud on the American consumer."

Winterkorn continued to deny wrongdoing. His trial in Germany was slated to start in September 2024. As for the American charges, Germany does not extradite citizens to the US.

* * *

The financial crisis of 2008 sparked the biggest economic crisis since the Great Depression. In the winter of 2008-2009 the US economy was losing 70,000 jobs a month. Within a year, the jobless rate had hit 10 percent. Nine million Americans would eventually lose their homes to foreclosure. Households lost trillions in net worth.

The human and economic misery was the result of corporate incompetence and ridiculous risk-taking by Wall Street firms, which were packaging bad housing loans and selling them to investors as mortgage-backed securities. In pursuit of profit, they had built a house of cards.

You can probably guess by now what happened to the perpetrators of this global disaster: none ended up in prison. The financial system was rescued by unprecedented bailouts of taxpayer money.

The financial sector is littered with examples of banks playing loose with the rules. Wells Fargo has paid billions in fines for its mortgage lending practices. BNP Paribas was ordered to pay $9 billion for sanctions violations. Deutsch Bank was fined $258 million for similarly violating international sanctions and paid $2.5 billion for manipulating interbank borrowing rates. In 2024, Canada's TD Bank was fined $3 billion over drug cartel money laundering. Attorney-General Merrick Garland said about TD, "by making its services convenient for criminals, it became one." However, I suspect that no senior executives at TD will be wearing orange jumpsuits anytime soon.

And there's Goldman Sachs, famously described by *Rolling Stone* as "a great vampire squid wrapped around the face of humanity, relentlessly jamming its blood funnel into anything that smells like money."

Goldman has been reprimanded over the last two decades for illegal behaviour with thirty-six citings resulting in over $10 billion in fines and settlements. Its infractions include corruption, aiding money laundering, trading ahead of clients, over-charging municipalities for government securities and for pay-to-play bribing of US state officials, to name just a few. In 2000, it paid $3.9 billion to settle a criminal probe over its role in the 1MBD scandal, which Reuters once labelled "one of the greatest financial heists in history."

Once again, in not one of these cases did executives go to prison. Middle America suffers but the bank senior executives keep their jobs, get promoted and get their bonuses even when the government has to bail them out. The fact that so many Americans suffered during the 2007-2008 financial crisis while the white-collar criminals walked away with big bonuses was in many ways the catalyst for the rise of populism in the US.

In his book *Too Big to Jail*, Virginia law professor Brandon Garrett compiled an impressive database of corporate prosecutions in the US between 2001 and 2014. He looked at 303 cases that ended in a DPA or fine. Individuals were charged in 34 percent of the cases and less than half of those ended with prison time.

In their defence, prosecutors argue they will gladly go after individuals when they can. But white-collar cases often present complexities and challenges: executives may be insulated by the structure of corporations (cases of willful blindness, for instance); they tend to have ample resources to defend themselves; and crimes often take place in foreign jurisdictions.

As Professor Garrett explained to the *New York Times*, "I've talked off the record to prosecutors. Some say they don't have the resources. It's one thing to settle with a big company and another thing to do serious investigations of dozens of people. Others say these aren't really intentional crimes, or it's difficult to establish intent in individual cases. Others just repeat the party line, which is, 'We target individuals whenever we have the evidence.' All of those are probably true to some extent."

The end result of so many of these cases is that nobody learns a lesson. When the odds are so high that nothing will personally happen to executives for their actions, there is little to deter them from doing bad things. A corporation paying a big fine is not really a motivating fear for an individual manager. If anything, deterrence is undermined.

I think that most CEOs would rather not be fired, but they don't mind when it happens. What they really don't want is to go to prison. I suspect that Telegram CEO Pavel Durov is second guessing his company's actions once he had to sit in a French jail. This will have a stronger deterrent impact than just going after the corporation which, after all, cannot go to jail. It also means that innocent parties such as employees are not as impacted.

It's important to look at these cases not to try to minimize what SNC-Lavalin did. Bribery is wrong but unlike the cases I have shared in this chapter the Libyan bribery scandal did not kill anyone. Just as our criminal system has very different penalties for murder and not paying your taxes we should treat bribery very differently than corporate malfeasance that results in hundreds of deaths. These cases also highlight that how the SNC-Lavalin case was handled fit a similar pattern in the world of white-collar crime. Countries, and certainly Canada in the case of SNC-Lavalin, have too often been treating the corporation as the criminal, not the people behind the crimes. The culpable individuals must be held accountable.

British Lord Chancellor Edward Thurlow famously said that corporations have "no soul to be damned, no body to kick." They can be reformed and remade, like SNC-Lavalin was, but they can't go to jail. At the same time, they are not driverless cars. They're run by people, sometimes motivated and blinded by greed.

12 | A done deal

At the end of 2019, after nearly a decade of legal and political drama the company plead guilty to charges that would ensure they were not debarred from government contracts.

It was a relief and welcome surprise, coming under a new justice minister handling a file that was still very much a hot potato. There had been a fear inside the company that it might take years in the court system to get the case resolved, if SNC-Lavalin even survived that long.

Under this new deal, a division of the company, SNC-Lavalin Construction, would plead guilty to fraud, pay a $280-million fine, and be subject to a three-year probation period.

From a reputational aspect, however, this was not great. Competitors could wave this guilty charge around and use it against the company. The charges against SNC-Lavalin Group Inc. and two of its other affiliates were dropped by the Crown.

This should have been solved years before, but the drama was finally over in the SNC-Lavalin scandal. The company had done wrong and key executives were behind it. The size of the fine was unprecedented, but fair. In fact, in our earlier efforts to settle the case, we had been willing to pay much more.

SNC-Lavalin would also welcome a monitor to keep tabs on the company's compliance efforts and file reports. Again, fair. But by now, pointless, given the world-class Compliance Department the company had created years ago under the watchful eye of World Bank monitor Joe Covington.

"The ironic thing," Neil Bruce told me, "is that SNC-Lavalin got essentially a bastardized DPA and paid less and had fewer restrictions than if the original DPA had been approved by public prosecutors."

In a press release from the Public Prosecution Service of Canada, Kathleen Roussel said only this: "I would like to thank the prosecutors for their dedicated work on this very challenging case, in the face of unprecedented public attention. They have demonstrated an unwavering commitment to ensuring a just outcome."

I certainly define "justice" differently than Roussel. In my version, the guilty do time and we protect the innocent. In this case, the guilty did no real time and it was the innocent employees and shareholders who were punished. Roussel would have been wise to consider that many laws are designed specifically not just to punish the guilty but protect the innocent. An example would be bankruptcy laws. A company might be in financial peril because of poor corporate leadership, but in bankruptcy, employee wages are given priority over other unsecured debts. Bankruptcy law also aims to help the company survive to protect as many jobs as possible. A DPA law has at its base the same principle: protect the innocent and punish the guilty. Unfortunately, Roussel didn't apply the law that had been passed by the government.

Sure, five years earlier this might have been a "just outcome." But I could not help but think: What did the government really get in the end? Had it done anything to deter future executives from committing similar crimes? I struggle to imagine another country trying so hard to tear down one of its few national champions.

Canada had taken one of its great success stories and reduced it to a shell of what it had once been. A company once on the verge of becoming the world's biggest engineering and construction firm was now a symbol of scandal. Punishment was doled out on innocent employees who had nothing to do with the crime, and investors—again, many of them Quebec pensioners. The company lost billions in contracts and spent eight years wrestling with a constant distraction.

And what about the actual criminals? Riadh Ben Aissa never spent a day in a Canadian prison over the Libya case. Only the Swiss incarcerated Ben Aissa. He had admitted to bribing foreign officials and stealing money from his employer. All told, an astounding $73,582,219 was funneled to Ben Aissa and to his predecessor, Sami Bebawi, "for their personal benefit," according to the Public Prosecution Service's own press release.

It was no accident that the stunning amount of money stolen by Ben Aissa and Bebawi was included in the details of the plea bargain. SNC-Lavalin managed to get this written in. It was a nod to the extreme criminal behavior that prosecutors had, in the case of Ben Aissa, virtually ignored.

Ben Aissa was never pursued with any of the zeal with which Roussel went after SNC-Lavalin. The crimes that had so offended Roussel and Wilson-Raybould's sense of justice did not seem to be that serious when the criminal was an individual, as opposed to a Canadian corporation.

In his work for the Crown as a "star witness" against SNC-Lavalin and Sami Bebawi, he used the oldest defence in the criminal handbook: everyone knew what he was doing, and he was just following orders. An obvious and blatant lie.

For his role in the Montreal hospital bribery case, Ben Aissa plead guilty to one charge of using a forged document. Fifteen other charges were dropped. His fifty-one-month prison sentence took into account his time served in another country, Switzerland, and time spent on conditional release. He ended up with what the judge called a "symbolic" one day of detention in Canada.

Ben Aissa was responsible for the theft of tens of millions of dollars, bribery and a case that crippled a Canadian icon, and he received one day in detention here in Canada. Yet there was no outrage to be found over this injustice.

Days before the SNC-Lavalin plea deal was announced, Bebawi was found guilty by a Quebec jury of fraud, corruption of a foreign public official, laundering proceeds of crime and possession of proceeds of crime. He was ordered to pay a fine of more than $24 million. He appealed the case but lost and in February 2023 was ordered to report to prison to serve his eight-year sentence. The seventy-six-year-old would be the only person to spend meaningful time behind bars in Canada over the case.

In early 2019, Pierre Duhaime pleaded guilty to helping a public official commit breach of trust in the McGill University Hospital case—essentially for acting with "willful blindness," as his lawyers put it in his statement of defense. He was sentenced to twenty months of house arrest, 240 hours of community service and ordered to make a $200,000 donation to a victims' fund. In the Libya case, he was never charged; there was never any suggestion he benefitted financially from Ben Aissa's theft.

Stéphane Roy was acquitted of charges over the Montreal hospital case. The fraud and bribery charges he faced in the Libya case were thrown out by the judge in February 2019 over unreasonable delays.

Cynthia Vanier spent eighteen months in a Mexican prison before she was released and the charges dropped. It might have been the harshest price paid by any of those involved. She had been wrapped up in an obviously harebrained plot. Vanier continued to defend herself vigorously against accusations of her involvement in the Gaddafi case. But her name—like Roy's, like Duhaime's, like Ben Aissa's—will forever be linked to the story.

The one positive outcome of the SNC-Lavalin affair is that Canada now does have a DPA law in place. This puts our companies on a level legal playing field with our other global major industrial competitors. I do believe that a company offered a DPA should be forced to change its CEO and a majority of its board of directors. We did more than that at SNC-Lavalin. We fired our CEO and any senior executives who had known or should have known about the Libyan or McGill University Hospital bribes. We also changed over the board completely. And I believe additionally companies offered DPAs should cooperate fully to ensure that the guilty individuals are prosecuted. We did that at SNC-Lavalin, but Canada's prosecutors had little interest in holding Riadh Ben Aissa, Stéphane Roy, and Pierre Duhaime accountable.

I can't help but wonder, at the end of the day, what would have happened if Canada had a DPA regime in place in 2012.

SNC-Lavalin would certainly have paid a huge fine. There would be no disputing that crimes had been committed and punishment was in order. It would have reported crimes to the government—just as it had done—because it was the right thing to do and also because, under the DPA regime, there would have been added incentive thanks to the self-reporting requirement.

There would have been a monitor put in place to make sure that the remediation was real and meaningful which the company had already done on its own in this case. SNC-Lavalin would have instituted a compliance program as the company did without any prompting from Canadian prosecutors. The company and its senior leadership would have been refreshed, just as they were.

Other things would have gone much differently. The government of Canada would not have spent hundreds of millions of dollars and several years pursuing criminal charges against the company. Hundreds of millions in shareholder value would not have been erased between 2012 and 2016. SNC-Lavalin would not have spent millions on additional legal fees. Thousands of SNC-Lavalin engineers in Canada would not have had to leave the firm and find other jobs. Many Canadian engineering graduates would have found jobs working for this great company. And the SNC-Lavalin name would not have been destroyed.

Most importantly, the government might have pursued the senior executives who were involved, starting with Riadh Ben Aissa, Sami Bebawi, and Pierre Duhaime. The outcomes of those cases would have served as meaningful deterrents to other business leaders: if you break the law, if you attempt to bribe, if you turn a blind eye to crimes under your watch, you will face harsh punishment. It will be the end of your career, and it could land you years in prison. I think that most CEOs would rather not be fired, but they don't mind when it happens. What they really don't want is to go to prison. That would have been a just outcome.

Who were the heroes of the story? The whistleblower who wrote the anonymous letter about Riadh Ben Aissa was one. The divisional finance director who flagged to the CFO that his business was being charged for expenses that were not approved for his business unit played his role well. Rejean Goulet, the company's general counsel, who forced Pierre Duhaime to bring the nefarious activities that had been uncovered to the board, was another. He stood up to his superiors and did the right thing, at risk to his job and career. Michael Sabia at the Caisse made sure that the company remained Canadian. There were also people like Brian Mulroney, Bill Morneau, and John Manley, who helped the company not because of some sinister plot to give slippery businesspeople a leg up, but because they thought it was the right thing to do for Canada.

And there were of course the employees who pushed on despite the overwhelming pressure put on them. They helped ensure that the company is still standing. That includes the CEOs (Bob Card, Neil Bruce, and Ian Edwards) who never gave up and whose persistence kept the ship afloat. And Erik Ryan, the company's head of government relations, who under three different CEOs never lost hope that a deal would get done that would save the company.

The villains are Ben Aissa, Pierre Duhaime, and Sami Bebawi, as well as the Gaddafis and Arthur Porter. Ben Aissa is probably the only one who walked away with ill-gotten gains, but he did not spend a day in jail in Canada. This is the saddest part of this entire affair. SNC-Lavalin did not get a DPA but for DPAs in the future to be an effective deterrent, we must ensure that the guilty individuals go to jail. To date, only twenty-five percent of DPAs prosecute the individuals involved. In my opinion that should be one hundred percent.

I also believe that both Jody Wilson-Raybould and Kathleen Roussel are villains in this story. I still struggle to understand how little interest they showed in weighing the bigger picture. Wilson-Raybould, in a pique of retribution against a Prime Minister who would not give her what she wanted on her most important file—Indigenous affairs—decided not to be a team player. Her inaction hurt many innocent people—namely the employees and shareholders. She should have remembered that she was the minister of justice for all Canadians.

Kathleen Roussel was treated as a hero but is certainly not that in my rendition of the story. She was a bureaucrat having no experience with DPAs who refused to listen to outside counsel and even some of her own people, deciding instead to destroy a Canadian company by not offering it a DPA. She got her facts wrong, as I have shown. In my view, she did not consider the Canadian public interest. Recall that 87 percent of Canadians agreed that it was not fair to punish innocent workers because of unethical practices by a small number of people. But at least she got her 15 minutes of fame.

Prime Minister Justin Trudeau was both hero and villain. A hero, because I think he was trying to do something that was good for all Canadians. As PM, he *should* be thinking about protecting jobs and helping Canadian companies thrive. That is why he so forcefully pushed to have a DPA law passed and then wanted it applied to SNC-Lavalin. The PM had nothing to gain pushing for a DPA settlement for SNC Lavalin. Not politically and certainly not personally. But based on their prior interactions, he should have understood that his justice minister was going to be a spoiler. His ham-fisted efforts to influence her to go his way were disastrous. He should have shuffled her out of justice way before this complicated issue was tackled.

Unfortunately, there were plenty of well-meaning people inside the company who went along to get along. I think that people who are part of a team succumb to this tendency. And the record shows us that stepping forward as a whistleblower is generally career suicide.

On January 28th, 1986 seven astronauts blasted off from Cape Canaveral including the first ever teacher to head to space, Christa McAuliffe. Millions of schoolchildren watched liftoff live. But just 73 seconds after liftoff the space shuttle Challenger blew up over the Atlantic Ocean. An investigation after the accident found the cause was failed o-ring seals in the space shuttle's right solid rock rocket booster that had been manufactured by Morton Thiokol. The company's own test data showed that the o-rings could fail in cold weather conditions similar to the temperature in Florida on January 28th. The Morton Thiokol engineers were overruled by management who were under pressure from NASA to launch as planned. One brave manager, Al McDonald, courageously bucked upper management and refused to sign the consent to launch authorization. His superior did sign and the launch unfortunately proceeded with catastrophic consequences. Al MacDonald was the key witness and whistleblower at the subsequent investigation into the crash. For speaking the truth he was demoted by the company.

Turning on a teammate isn't just a hard thing to do, it's often considered the wrong thing. Do you have your teammate's back, or do you report them? A case in point is again Boeing, whose troubles we discussed in Chapter 11. John Barnett had worked at Boeing for thirty years and he left the company after he had been harassed for logging a whistleblower complaint about safety concerns. The company made life difficult for him and after two days of testimony he shot himself in his truck. Had they listened to John two horrific crashes might have been prevented.

At West Point, the US Military Academy, there is a cadet honour code: "A Cadet will not lie, cheat, steal, or tolerate those who do." The rule is clear. If you see a fellow cadet doing something wrong, you turn them in. One of the best books on leadership that I read during my time in the Army was *Crisis in Command* by Richard Gabriel and

Paul Savage. It laid out the failures in leadership during the Vietnam War. The authors emphasize the problem with West Point's Code: "the objection that the Academy's honor code, especially the non-toleration clause, turns all 'brother officers' into potential stool pigeons is a real one. The prerequisite of any successful cooperative institution such as an officer corps is to inculcate within the individual officer a sense of what is to be done and what is not to be done. This most certainly does not require that every member of the corps keep watch on the behavior of every other officer, or that an officer's unethical conduct be betrayed to his superiors." The authors go on to explain that "a common occurrence and one which brings wry smiles to the faces of experienced officers is to see a young West Point graduate report another officer for an honor offence!"

This non-toleration clause is a not a part of the code at the Royal Military College of Canada. If that code had existed at RMC, I'm pretty sure I would have been kicked out as I often overlooked minor rule infractions committed by my peers. This does not mean letting major infractions go unpunished, but building a team does sometimes mean looking out for a buddy. A cop who backs up a peer who is late with a lame excuse is different from one who lies to protect a peer who shot an unarmed innocent person.

In Larouche's book, Gilles Laramee, SNC-Lavalin's former CFO, discussed the challenge of breaking ranks. "It is nice to be able to denounce. There are people who are formidable, as I told the RCMP, who are seven-foot-four and are able to denounce everything, who are able to do everything. I did not. I regret that."

Gilles is probably right when he says that most people might not have stood up to their bosses and so we should applaud those brave souls who do. People like Al McDonald at Morton Thiokol, John Barnett at Boeing, and Facebook whistleblower Frances Haugen, who went to the US Congress to lay out how her employer was putting profits ahead of safety. Or the brave Cassidy Hutchinson who testified before the US January 6 Commission about President Trump's behavior. Or my former boss, Mitt Romney, who stood as the lone Republican to vote for the first Trump impeachment, thus becoming the first senator in US history to vote to remove a president of his own party from office. We need more leaders like Mitt Romney and Liz Cheney who are willing to put country ahead of self. We need more of these seven-foot-four people with the spines to call out wrongdoing.

There is little doubt that more people within SNC-Lavalin than let on knew that Riadh Ben Aissa's dealings in the Middle East were shady. Why didn't more come forward? They weren't unusual. A May 2024 Gallup survey found that less than half of employees (forty-three percent) who had first-hand awareness of unethical behavior within their organization in the past twelve months actually reported it, either directly or through an anonymous tip.

I recently attended the fortieth reunion for my business school class and participated in a great session with Harvard Professor Max Bazerman, who wrote *Complicit: How we Enable the Unethical and How to Stop*. Bazerman laid out numerous examples of wrongdoing where many complicit people did not come forward. These highly public examples include Harvey Weinstein, Jeffrey Epstein, Michigan State University (where Dr. Larry Nassar abused over 265 identified victims) and the Catholic Church. He also spent a great deal of time discussing the Theranos case. This was the company in California led by the charismatic Elizabeth Holmes who claimed her company had developed a machine that could carry out numerous medical tests using a very small blood sample. Many people within Theranos knew that the machines did not work. Despite this, the company's high-profile board, featuring such luminaries as Henry Kissinger, James Mattis, and George Shultz were taken in, as were numerous venture capitalists and the Walgreens drug store chain. How were they fooled? Part of the reason, he says, is that human nature is to trust other people. At SNC-Lavalin, the board certainly trusted Pierre Duhaime. He had had a long and successful career in the company with a clean rap sheet.

At Theranos only four of the eight hundred employees became whistleblowers. A brave junior employee, Tyler Shultz (the grandson of Theranos director and former Secretary of State George Shultz) was one of them. Why did others not step forward? And why did others not raise the caution flag at SNC-Lavalin?

I suspect it was loyalty to the people above them. It was probably also respect for the 100-year-old institution of which they were very proud. Professor Bazerman points out that "psychologists refer to our inability to see bad in people and organizations to whom we are loyal as an aspect of motivated blindness." He goes on to say that "in the realm of complicity, bias toward inaction is exacerbated by uncertainty. When we aren't certain that someone is engaged in unethical activity but think they probably are, the idea of accusing them feels risky, awkward, and potentially harmful. After all, what if we're wrong? Our uncertainty leads us to say nothing and become complicit. But rather than accepting this uncertainty and moving on, we should be motivated to learn more."

Several key managers at SNC-Lavalin should have been motivated to learn more about Riadh Ben Aissa's actions.

In some cases, people were complicit because it was in their personal interest. Pierre Duhaime went along with Ben Aissa's schemes because as the company's profits grew, he personally gained. It was probably also a case of "Mind your own business" or "It is not my job to tattle on others." As mentioned, being a whistleblower is also not generally career enhancing. The key is to make sure that people are rewarded for coming forward—but that is easier said than done.

Many years ago, I was a finalist for a Rhodes Scholarship and the last step in the process was to be interviewed by a panel of prominent Canadians. One of my panelists was Pauline Jewett, the NDP Member of Parliament. She asked me whether I would have followed orders had I been a soldier at My Lai, which was the horrific massacre of women and children in Vietnam in 1968. I told her categorically that I not only would not have followed those orders but that I would have reported this criminal activity up the chain of command. I pointed out that the Code of Military Discipline only requires one to follow lawful orders and the killing of innocent women and children is certainly not lawful. Most soldiers I served with would have done the right thing. I also believe that most people in business also strive to do the right thing.

As well as heroes and villains, there were real victims in the SNC-Lavalin affair. As I've noted a number of times, shareholders paid a high price (including six million Quebec depositors at the Caisse). So did taxpayers, who saw their government waste hundreds of millions pursuing a case over seven years that could have been resolved in less than eighteen months.

Now where do I fit in this hero-villain-victim storyline? I think I was all three at various times. I was a victim of Riadh Ben Aissa, like everyone else. And a villain in that I played a role in promoting Pierre

Duhaime. Finally, like the rest of my fellow board members, a hero, in that we stayed with the ship in heavy storms and saw the company through to calmer seas.

There are things I would have done differently, in hindsight. Not fighting the World Bank's sanctions was one mistake. Bob Card's Eagle Scout plan seemed like the right thing to do at the time. And we thought Canadian officials, investors, and the public at large would take note that we were doing the hard work to set things straight as quickly as possible.

But the company got no credit for this at all from Canadian prosecutors. Instead, the guilty plea was used against it. Coverage of the case focused on how SNC-Lavalin had received the stiffest penalty ever doled out by the World Bank.

The better course of action would have been to fight the flimsy charges. Even if true, they were small cases of bribery, the kinds of things that were virtually inescapable for any large global company. We would have won (the case did fall apart in the end), and the litigation would have been confidential. The narrative would not have been that SNC-Lavalin had committed fraud. The director of public prosecutions would not have been able to use the company's "past corruption in other countries" as justification for denying it a remediation agreement.

Time and again we seemed to find ourselves on the wrong side of public opinion. In the early phases of our efforts to get a DPA regime, we tried to keep our head down publicly and talk to the people that mattered in Ottawa. By the time the political scandal hit, unfortunately, all the stories about SNC-Lavalin were stunningly negative. We'd missed the chance to get our side of the story out, that we were not an evil company, but the victim of a handful of bad actors.

I wish we'd been more open and proactive early on. We didn't explain well enough the big steps we'd taken: undertaking serious compliance efforts, firing employees connected to wrongdoing, remaking of our corporate culture, self-reporting, and cooperating with the RCMP. Even what SNC-Lavalin was doing in Libya in the first place was too often misunderstood. No one remembered the version of Gaddafi who was embraced by world leaders. Or that businesses like SNC-Lavalin were being encouraged to invest there.

There are some concrete steps the board could have taken, too. There should have been stronger centralized financial controls. That could have included updates to the board about agency fee payments. We should have had a compliance department in place much earlier than we did. (For more on this see the Epilogue, "Ten ideas on corporate governance.") Steps like these might possibly have raised red flags about Raidh Ben Aissa.

They certainly would have provided an important check on the risks inherent in SNC-Lavalin's eat-what-you-kill corporate culture. Had we, as leaders, ignored those risks? It's hard to know the genesis of the corruption that infected SNC-Lavalin. "There is a chicken and egg aspect to this," one of the lawyers involved in the case told me recently. "Was the primary driver for corruption Ben Aissa's desire to supplement his generous compensation package with money that needed to come from a shady set-up for foreign agent payments, or was the 'company leadership' requiring success at any cost and Ben Aissa/Bebawi went along for the ride as enablers and double-dipped for themselves to compensate for the risks they were taking for SNC?"

Ultimately, the question of how much blame lies at the feet of board members is a tough one to answer.

In a 2013 op-ed in the *Globe and Mail*, then-chairman Gwyn Morgan asked, "Could the board have done more to detect the wrongdoings that have since come to light? The answer to that question is as troubling to SNC-Lavalin board members as it must be to all corporate directors."

At heart, there was a problem. "Non-executive directors are not involved in day-to-day operations of the company. They must rely on information received from people within the company. When a small number of people deliberately set out to falsify documents, commit bribery and cover up theft, it can be exceedingly difficult to detect, even with good controls in place. This has proven to be true at corporations around the world."

Apart from these hard-earned lessons in management, my experience at SNC-Lavalin also coloured my view of Canada's industrial policy, which has consistently failed to encourage domestic business and investment.

In the SNC-Lavalin case, it was amateur hour. Canada went after a domestic global leader with laws that dramatically punished its own companies. Foreign companies could do exactly what SNC-Lavalin had done and quickly recover using DPAs in their home countries.

There are plenty of ways to improve Canada's corporate competitiveness. As a basic starting point, we need policies that encourage domestic investment and the growth of globally competitive companies. SNC-Lavalin won contracts around the world to build hydro dams and aluminum smelters thanks to the knowledge built here. And yet far too often the only factor Canada considers in bids is cost, not the value of building strong domestic companies capable of competing globally. And yet this is what other nations do every day.

Try winning a contract for significant military procurement in the US or in France, where SNC-Lavalin competed for years but was never able to win any large-scale government contracts. These were generally awarded to domestic champions. Back in the early 1990s, CAE, where I sat on the board, was unable to win major fighter jet simulator contracts in the US despite being the worldwide leader in advanced flight simulation.

Canada, meanwhile, plays by Marquess of Queensberry rules and allows virtually unfettered access to the Canadian market to foreign firms that make no long-term investments here.

Years ago, when I was in the book business at Chapters, our competitor adorned many of their stores with the slogan, "The World Needs More Canada." The world does need more Canada but often Canada helps foreigners more than it helps domestic businesses. Amazon was able to ship books from the US to Canada and not charge taxes while we as a Canadian company could not do that. Amazon was able to use US book wholesalers such as Ingram to fulfill its Canadian orders, but as a Canadian bookseller we could not do the same. Thus, Ingram could fulfill customer orders in a couple of days while we had to wait weeks to get these same books from the Canadian distributors (who were given monopoly control of titles by the Canadian government). When I tried to set up a Canadian book wholesaler, Pegasus, that would allow Chapters to offer delivery times comparable to Amazon's, the Canadian government held us up for nine months. This was done to protect Canadian publishers, many of whom are now either gone or US-owned. In 2024, BookNet Canada reported that Canadian-owned publishers accounted for only 5.3 percent of English language trade books. Today in the retail trade, Amazon dominates the Canadian book industry.

I have generally found that politicians of all three major parties and the mainstream media in Canada are generally anti-big business. They are in favor of business if it's the small corner convenience store, but it is a national sport to attack any successful large enterprise or large Canadian companies such as the banks, cable companies, and telcos. The "tall poppy" syndrome at work.

Both the media and political parties are reflecting what Canadian voters want. Canada is, after all, a left-of-center country. For ninety-three of the past 129 years, Canada has been run by the Liberal Party. Since the Second World War the parties of the left in Canada have won, on average, sixty percent of the national vote. It would be useful for all Canadians to understand that our standard of living and our social programs are actually based on having successful Canadian global competitors. We should all be cheering for our national business champions.

I will share one example to highlight the challenge we face vis-à-vis our direct competitors in the United States. When I first stepped in to be the CEO of Pep Boys in Philadelphia I had to make major decisions quickly. This was a turn-around situation. This $2-billion company was bleeding cash and owed hundreds of millions of dollars in debt, much of which had to be repaid in the next eighteen months. My first decision, just two weeks after taking the helm was that we would have to lay off more than one thousand people in our stores and in the support office so that we could stop the negative cash flow.

I met with Pep Boys' public relations firm so that we could discuss the messages that we would communicate to the market. Based on my Canadian experience, I told them that the next day when we announced the layoffs we would be hit with very negative press. This would certainly have been the case had this been a story in Toronto. They disagreed with me and said it would actually be a good news story. That's exactly how it played the next day in the *Philadelphia Inquirer*, with a headline about a new CEO who was revitalizing this important business.

The sad spectacle of the SNC-Lavalin affair should help us understand that it is not in our national interest to treat our companies worse than their foreign competitors are treated. Great iconic companies like Goldman Sachs, Siemens, Airbus, Wal-Mart, PWC, McKinsey, Volkswagen, Boeing, Pfizer and Ericsson have all been slapped for unethical practices, sometimes more than once, and yet in every single case their brands stand strong today as their governments acted to swiftly get the ship righted. Not so in Canada with SNC-Lavalin. The long-drawn-out scandal left a more than 100-year-old brand tarnished.

* * *

On September 18, 2023, SNC-Lavalin changed its name to AtkinsRéalis. The company was still struggling. The new CEO, Ian Edwards, had sought to simplify the business, focusing on engineering services and consulting, and selling off oil and gas assets. The stock price was on the rise but stuck around where it had been in 2012, when we were first learning about the activities of Ben Aissa and Cynthia Vanier and Stéphane Roy. The case and its mishandling had set the company back a good eight to ten years.

The name change struck me as a sensible move. In fact, the board had argued after the acquisition of Atkins that SNC-Lavalin should consider changing its name to Atkins. We ultimately decided that it should wait until the charges had been settled. Atkins had its own history and name recognition. It was a banner the company could move forward under. But it marked the end of the SNC-Lavalin brand.

Actualité asked the question in a February 8, 2019 article that captures the primary thesis of this book. The prosecutor should have pursued the much better path which was a DPA. They said "Knowing the economic and political consequences of refusing to negotiate an out of court settlement, and knowing that a possibility exists, and is legal, and is practiced around the world, why not pursue that avenue." That DPA avenue was open to the prosecutor but for her own unique reasons she chose a very different and perilous route.

I'll end at the very beginning of the SNC-Lavalin story: The origin of the company is something that deserves to be celebrated. Like the Canadarm or Blackberry or Nortel, it's one of those rare business successes where Canada broke new ground and, for a moment at least, sat on top of the world.

In 1911, Arthur Surveyer, a thirty-two-year-old engineer, opened a small consulting firm. He'd decided to strike out on his own after working for several years with the federal government in the public works department. He opened up shop on Saint-François-Xavier Street in Montreal, the same street where his father owned a hardware store. The office was crowded, crammed with books and lit by gas lamps. His principles were simple, said Camille Dagenais, SNC-Lavalin's CEO from 1967 to 1975. "You have to be the best in what you do and that your client has to be completely satisfied with what you're doing."

One of his first big contracts was to design and supervise the construction of a hydropower station near Grand-Mere, Quebec. Little did he know that from this humble start SNC would, over the next century, design and build many of the largest hydropower projects in the world.

SNC focused on those industrial sectors where Quebec was strong and then used the experience and knowledge they gained to complete projects further afield. Surveyer got his first international contract in 1921 for an engineering study for a pulp mill in Aberdeen, in the state of Washington.

In the 1930s, Surveyer took on two partners, Emil Nenniger and Georges Chênevert, and the firm's name was eventually changed to Surveyer, Nenniger & Chênevert. That ultimately morphed into SNC.

The trio expanded into many industry sectors where Quebec was a global player, including aluminum and mining. Their first aluminum smelter engineering work was done for the American Aluminum Company in Arvida, Quebec. Their first significant mining contract was to design a chromium smelter in Sault Ste. Marie. By 1990 it was a $300-million engineering company.

The merger with Lavalin followed, as did the incredible growth through the 2000s. Surveyer's little shop now operated in virtually every corner of the world, building transit systems, airports, ferry terminals, bridges, buildings, water treatment facilities, pipelines, mines, and nuclear power plants.

It was a remarkable company until it was pulled apart little by little, by the people—including government officials—who should have been busy building it up.

Through the perseverance and the hard work of thousands of employees this tarnished icon wasn't completely levelled. And it's thanks to them that it is rising again.

Epilogue: Ten ideas on corporate governance

In the years since the SNC-Lavalin affair, I often get asked by colleagues in the business world what lessons I learned as a board director there. Surely, they claim, there must have been *something* that the board could have done to prevent this tragedy. Many probably say to themselves that the board should have been able to smell the smoke from the blaze that was about to engulf the company.

It's a perspective handily captured in something that Patricia Adams, the executive director of Probe International, a government and corporate watchdog based in Toronto—who to the best of my knowledge has never served on a public company board—said to the CBC about SNC-Lavalin's directors during the scandal: "What's your role on the board if not to protect the corporation from acts of bribery and from doing things that are illegal?"

That is easy to say, but very hard to do when your CEO and two other key executives are deliberately hiding facts from board members.

I have served on seventeen public and private company boards over the past thirty years. During that time, I have been the chair of three public company boards and seven private company boards. I have served and chaired virtually every committee of a public company board. I genuinely believe that I have the experience to challenge the pundits and academic gurus who question the integrity and leadership of the SNC-Lavalin board in 2011 and 2012, when the wrongdoing occurred and was uncovered.

I admit I am not an unbiased observer. I was on the board at the time. But I remain convinced that it was excellent and did its job as well as any board in Canada. It is worth remembering that for many consecutive years the SNC-Lavalin board was independently rated in the top ten percent in Canada for governance.

In fact, in 2009, just two years before the proverbial shit hit the fan, the SNC-Lavalin board was rated as the absolute best board in Canada by the *Globe and Mail* out of more than two hundred public companies. This was not a one-time occurrence. The firm had also been rated as the best in Canada in 2005, had finished second in the 2006 rankings, and third in 2008.

In 2011, the very year of the troubles, SNC-Lavalin received the award for Corporate Governance from the Canadian Institute of Chartered Accountants, the seventh time in the previous ten years that the company had been so honoured.

So, how could such an impressive board suddenly fail so completely in its duty? The answer is that it didn't. The SNC-Lavalin board did its job. It acted expeditiously as soon as it discovered that something was amiss. I personally had fifty-six board and committee meetings in the eighteen-month period starting in late 2011. The board took decisive action to replace the guilty executive officers and quickly jumped in with both feet to keep the ship afloat in very turbulent times. It fired the CEO, named an interim team, and hired third party forensic investigators to get the facts. The board also went above and beyond to make sure that the authorities were fully informed at the same time that the board were made aware of facts.

Those who have served on public company boards will know that it is virtually impossible for a board to prevent wrongdoing when it is orchestrated by very few senior executives. Especially if the CEO is one of those executives.

Back in March 2000 the two leaders of Cinar, the producer of many television shows including *Arthur*, invested $179 million without the approval of the board. Micheline Charest and her husband Ronald Weinberg, as well as CFO Hasanain Panju, were accused of using the company as their personal piggy bank. How does something like that happen? Well, the board is not on site every day and they have to leave the management of the company to the CEO and their team.

But directors are ultimately responsible since they represent the shareholders, and they select the CEO. So logically if the CEO makes illegal moves, the board must hold itself accountable.

This highlights the need for boards to pick CEOs they can trust to direct the business legally and ethically. In my business career I have worked closely with more than two hundred CEOs and, aside from SNC Lavalin, only one other of those CEOs engaged in illegal activity. At the start of my career with Bain and Co. in London one of our clients was Guinness, the beer company. Ernest Saunders, the CEO of Guinness, attempted to fraudulently manipulate the share price of Guinness in his takeover bid for Distillers. He was sentenced to five years in prison.

I submit that more than ninety-nine percent of CEOs would never consider doing something illegal. The challenge is that a few select outliers can badly damage a company and its employees and shareholders, as happened at SNC-Lavalin. For this and many other reasons, CEO selection is one of the core functions of the board and a topic I will return to later.

Having said that the SNC-Lavalin board did an excellent job does not mean that there weren't actions that might not have helped discover danger sooner. Like the Monday recording of a Sunday football game, there are certainly plays that can be picked apart to see what could be improved on.

Here are my ten key takeaways on corporate governance.

1. Board Composition

When I first went on boards some thirty years ago, they were primarily drawn from the "old boys" network. It was a club of folks who knew each other well and had decades of business experience. Most were, or had been, senior executives (mostly CEOs).

The pros of this arrangement were that these were people with relevant experience who by and large were not dependent on the income they earned from sitting on boards. Directors might be on three or four, and were not expected to attend every single meeting.

The requirements were not particularly onerous. As well, given their stature in the business world, combined with the fact that serving as a director was not their main source of income, these directors were very willing to stand up to any Type A personality serving as CEO.

Fast forward to today and I would argue that there are too many directors who cannot go toe-to-toe with the typical aggressive CEO. Many directors have never been CEOs. In fact, Spencer Stuart, the headhunting firm, reports in its Directors Pulse 2024 Survey, only thirty percent of directors in 2024 were either active or retired CEOs. As well, many of today's directors now depend on their directorships for their income. They are thus much less willing to challenge the hyper-confident CEO at the helm. Charles Elson, the founding Director of the Weinberg Center for Corporate Governance, points out that directors "know their bread is buttered by the CEO and they will do anything—and go through any hoops to justify their decisions" (to support the CEO). We need more directors who will stand up to the CEO.

Every board desperately needs one or two PITA (pain in the ass) directors. These directors may not win popularity contests, but they are willing to challenge management and their fellow directors when groupthink sets in.

For example, Avie Tevanian, a director at Theranos, asked to see the contracts the company had with pharma companies. Tevanian was concerned that CEO Elizabeth Holmes kept talking about lucrative contracts but somehow the revenue never seemed to follow. Tevanian had made money at Apple and invested $1.5 million in Theranos and served on the board of directors. He went to the board chairman, Don Lucas, to complain, but the chair sided with the CEO. Avie left the board. The company disappeared and Holmes was convicted of wire fraud and conspiracy and sentenced to eleven years.

The chair should have listened. It is these PITA directors—the kinds of people who can help get the answers—that a board needs. Shortly after becoming chairman at SNC-Lavalin, I brought one such PITA director onto the board. He was experienced and was always willing to ask the tough questions.

Boards do need the full range of expertise, but the key expertise required is business acumen and judgment based on years of experience. It might be nice to have an environmental expert on the board, for instance, but I would contend the most critical elements on a board are people who are courageous and willing to stand up for the shareholders.

SNC-Lavalin had several directors who were or had been very successful CEOs of large complex organizations including Pierre Lessard the former CEO of Metro and Claude Mongeau, who at the time was the CEO of CN. They brought enormous talent, expertise, and courage to their roles as directors. Directors should also be willing to resign if need be to make sure stakeholders are protected. SNC Lavalin had several of these principled directors.

I believe that boards should never be larger than eleven members and, if possible, nine is an even better target. Small boards can work together more effectively and collaboratively to build rapport.

Boards also need new blood to stay fresh and relevant. Many boards now have term and/or age limits (Hugessen Consulting reports that one-third of boards have either age or term limits). I am strongly in favor of term limits but think any age limit, if needed, should be much higher than seventy-four, which many boards now use. I know of many seventy-nine-year-olds who could continue to bring enormous experience and wisdom to many boards. Who would not want to have had either Charlie Munger or, today, Warren Buffett on their board? Term limits accomplish the same purpose as age limits, but are better in ensuring board renewal (as an aside, I think term limits would also help for political renewal!).

The best way to renew boards, and simultaneously make them stronger and more effective, is through rigorously evaluating the individual directors. Most boards do some version of this but frankly, it is often more to check a compliance box than truly build a better board. A director should get feedback not only from the chairperson and other directors but also should get feedback from the senior executive team. This is particularly relevant as a 2024 annual survey conducted by PWC highlighted that only 30 percent of executives rated their board's performance as good or excellent.

Every board I have ever served on has had at least one or two weaker directors, and they should have been asked to resign by the chairman. A 2022 survey by PwC, the accounting and consulting giant, of seven hundred public company directors in the US found that half of directors said that at least one director needed to be replaced. This seems low in my opinion.

Underperforming directors stay on until their term is up. A strong chairman, with the help of honest feedback from the other directors on the board, should be able to deal with underperforming directors. When I stepped into the role of chair at SNC-Lavalin, one of the first steps we took was to hire a third-party evaluator. This evaluator spoke to each director for more than an hour to get feedback on all the other directors. This gave me and the Chair of the Governance Committee the data we needed to refresh the board and to make it more effective overall. Unfortunately, according to Spencer Stuart, only 28 percent of boards use this type of third-party evaluation.

The best board I ever served on when it came to evaluating directors was Sobeys, the grocery chain. Each year, every director ranked all the directors' effectiveness. Those rankings, showing each director's standing from strongest to weakest, were shared with the entire board. John Bragg, the great entrepreneur who built a business empire, was often rated as the best director. When John spoke, it was usually important, and everyone listened. But this rigorous process also led to several weaker directors self-selecting themselves off the board. Most boards know full well which directors contribute most to the oversight and leadership of the enterprise.

2. Board Diversity

Boards benefit enormously from diversity. This is true for all types of diversity. In the interest of brevity let me focus on gender diversity.

When I first started serving on boards, many were all male. There was certainly a significant amount of male bias at the time which led to women being underrepresented on boards. But it also had much to do with the fact that many women had not yet accumulated decades of senior management experience. According to Leanin.org women accounted for just five percent of Fortune 500 CEOs in 2015, but that had doubled to ten percent by 2024. Women represented seventeen percent of C Suite members in 2015. By 2024 it was 29 percent. There are now many more women with the experience it takes to serve on boards.

I am convinced that all boards gain as a result of gender diversity. Women now have had significant amounts of senior executive experience and, in addition to having the same skillset as their male counterparts, they bring several unique perspectives to any board. The most important that I have seen is intuitive people judgement. This is obviously a generalization, but women seem to have a superior ability to assess character traits that are difficult-to-define or evaluate quickly.

The SNC-Lavalin board was a perfect laboratory in this regard. The board at the time of the troubles was made up of eight men and three women. During my time there, the board had to make two critical decisions that were fundamentally about character, These were decisions based on a very individual and subjective assessment. In both cases the men's judgment was not as accurate as the women's. All three women voted in the way that history will judge to have been correct.

I realize that the data point of one company does not make a rule, but I have been on other public company boards that were initially all-male when I joined but then added female directors. In all cases this made the boards stronger and provided a new dimension to virtually every board discussion.

In 2024, I attended a six-week course on Artificial Intelligence at MIT. In one class we learned how to make groups smarter in making decisions. MIT's research showed that three factors were critical in group decision-making effectiveness. The first factor was the average social intelligence and perceptiveness of the group. This is essentially a variant of EQ or emotional intelligence. The second factor was treating all members of the group equally (I will return to this latter when discussing the role of the chairman). The third factor, according to MIT, was the number of women in the group. That is because women are better at the first factor, social perceptiveness.

MIT's research makes clear that it is hard to judge the group's average social intelligence, but a good proxy is, "How many women are in the group?" I am certainly not into quotas but believe that women make a board stronger. That was the case at SNC-Lavalin.

3. Chairperson-CEO Relationship

The first rule of good governance is that the chair and CEO positions should not be held by one person. The chair and the CEO have very different roles to play. The roles have been held by two different people at SNC-Lavalin for decades. The CEO runs the business and the chair presides over the board, which is the CEO's boss. Each must stay in their lane.

The chair and the board have vital roles in governance, approving strategy, and hiring and firing CEOs, but they are not the day-to-day managers. The most important relationship on the board is that between the chairperson and the CEO. The chairperson is there to help guide the CEO. This is especially important for a new CEO. At SNC-Lavalin, in the critical period, the chairperson was based on the West Coast at a time when we had a new CEO. It certainly would have helped had the chair been geographically closer to the CEO to allow for more frequent in-person interactions. In our new "virtual world" these in-person interactions are even more important.

It takes time for a chairperson and a CEO to develop a relationship to allow them to trust one another. When I first joined the board I could see that Guy Saint-Pierre as chairman and Jacques Lamarre as CEO were able to develop that relationship based on years of working together. That best practice of a trusting longstanding relationship did obviously not exist at the time of the troubles at SNC-Lavalin.

In our portfolio companies at Clearspring Capital, I make sure that early on I invest heavily to build a strong relationship with my CEOs. This means we talk weekly but more importantly; we have a monthly dinner with a completely open agenda. The CEO should feel comfortable discussing sensitive business and personnel issues with the chair. Often the chairperson will have the experience to help coach the CEO.

This is especially true for new CEOs. When I became the board chair at SNC-Lavalin I invested significant time to build strong relationships with both Bob Card and then Neil Bruce. This meant we visited construction sites around the world together, which gave us time to build trust. We also had dinner one-on-one each month with an open agenda.

I also made sure I had a pass key and an office in the SNC-Lavalin headquarters. I enjoyed walking around and meeting folks and this resulted in staff often dropping into my office to just chat. This often gave me insights about the issues facing the business, many of which we then discussed at subsequent board meetings.

I try to do the same thing with our portfolio companies at Clearspring Capital. As employees a few levels below the CEO get to know me, they are much more apt to let me know what is happening in the field. This "upward feedback" led to me parting ways with one of our CEOs but more often these sources of information help me to coach our CEOs to make them more effective.

4. CEO Selection

The selection of the CEO of a company is one of the most important roles a board must play. David Beatty, a well-known Board governance expert, who has been the Chair of eight publicly traded companies, states that "the board's most scared trust is picking the CEO." I agree wholeheartedly. One can certainly argue given what happened under Pierre Duhaime's leadership that the SNC-Lavalin board failed when it chose him to succeed Jacques Lamarre. For many years I ran a program with military veterans that taught leadership at the Ivey Business School and to senior executives. My lecture highlighted that leaders excel generally in three areas which I called the three Cs. First any leader must be competent. That is true whether you are a military leader or a business executive. Napoleon, Alexander the Great, and Rommel were all very competent military leaders. Satya Nadella, the CEO of Microsoft, and Airbnb CEO Brian Chesky have proven their competence in leading their organizations. Second a leader must master communication. This means being able to clearly articulate a vision for where you want your followers to go and then be able to motivate them to want to go there. In politics Churchill was a master communicator as were both Presidents Clinton and Obama. The final area that is critical to effective leadership is by far the most important and that is character. Character includes courage, empathy, loyalty, and integrity. The most important character trait is that the leader should do the right thing. Clearly this attribute was missing in some of the very key executives at SNC-Lavalin.

Ideally the outgoing CEO would have provided at least a few choices of internal candidates for promotion to the CEO role. Research by Spencer Stuart, looked at 300 CEO transitions and found that insiders were better for shareholder returns and growth in revenue and profit than outside hires (except when the firm was in trouble). SNC-Lavalin was in strong shape when it was time to find a new CEO to replace Jacques Lamarre. He had prepared well in the period leading to his retirement. The board initially had four internal candidates. Two of the candidates ran major divisions within the company. One of the other candidates was the chief financial officer and the final candidate very successfully led SNC-Lavalin Capital, which was the business unit that invested in assets such as Altalink and the 407 highway.

The leader of SNC-Lavalin Capital left to join another business, which left us with three candidates. As the chairman of the board's human resources committee, I was very involved in the discussions as to how we should select the best CEO from these final three candidates.

I wish we had followed a process that we did at CAE, where I also chaired the HR committee. CAE had two outstanding candidates to fill in for the retiring Bob Brown. In that case we sent both candidates to a four-day assessment, which was not only helpful to the board in making the final selection but was also helpful to the individuals by giving them a very accurate assessment of the things they would need to do to be more effective CEOs when they were in the seat.

This evaluation included comprehensive 360 evaluations. A 360 evaluation means that an executive is evaluated not only by his boss but also by his direct reports and his or her peers.

I have always been a strong advocate for them. At the Royal Military College, we were evaluated using 360 evaluations that included peer evaluations twice a year. This was a critical development tool for all of us. We could see how our peers saw us. Bain & Company was also a fervent convert to the value of 360 evaluations as all leaders did an OMBA (Officer Manager Behavioral Assessment) twice a year. Socrates said that to know thyself is the beginning of wisdom. My favourite Scot, Robbie Burns, said "*o wad some pow'r the giftie gie us to see oursels as ithers see us.*"

These 360 evaluations give us exactly that power to see ourselves as others see us. We can then honestly work on those things that we need to improve. The most important feedback I got as CEO of Chapters was my annual evaluation from all my direct reports.

In retrospect, I do wish we had sent the SNC-Lavalin candidates for that assessment and had done 360 evaluations as well, as these might have had an impact on our final selection and would certainly have provided some guidance to the person we selected to be CEO, Pierre Duhaime.

Interestingly, a few years later, when we were considering Bob Card's replacement at SNC-Lavalin and I was the chairman, we did send our top two candidates to the same CEO evaluation program in the United States.

The outgoing CEO should not be part of the final decision in choosing the next CEO. His input to the board on this topic is vital, but a strong CEO can have a disproportionate impact on the selection process. I witnessed this same phenomenon on another board where a CEO played much too significant a role in choosing his favoured successor. When his chosen internal candidate was not chosen, the retiring CEO asked for a do-over so that his chosen one could get another shot at being selected for the job. The retiring CEO will no longer be there (in fact should no longer remain on the board after retiring as CEO) – the responsibility for choosing the next CEO rests with the board.

5. Strong Centralized Financial Controls

Jacques Lamare had built a very decentralized company at SNC-Lavalin. He strongly believed that business unit heads should get to run their own businesses with little direct oversight from staff functions.

This applied to finances as well. The financial director of each division had a direct reporting relationship to the division head but really only a dotted line relationship to the company's chief financial officer. The divisional finance directors understood that the division head, and not the CFO, called the shots.

I strongly believe that this structure was one of the reasons that Riadh Ben Aissa and Stéphane Roy, who was his financial officer, were able to divert funds the way they did at SNC-Lavalin. A much stronger central financial function would have been able to oversee and prevent the actions that these two individuals took.

In my private equity role, we make sure that there are very strong centralized financial controls. There is no excuse for a company CFO to not know where large sums of money are going. We ensure that every CFO is signing the CFO certificate every quarter that makes clear that we have accurate and complete financial statements. I point out to our CFOs that they should think that they are signing those statements in blood.

Additionally, in my opinion, internal audit should report directly to the audit committee. This was not the case at SNC-Lavalin, although the board's audit committee did meet regularly with the internal auditor in-camera.

I also think the audit committee should generally meet with the CFO without the CEO present. As the CEO of both Chapters and Pep Boys, I never attended audit committee meetings unless the chair of the audit committee specifically asked for me to join them for specific agenda items. The CEO too often fields the questions when in reality the CFO should be able to respond to all the issues related to the company's financial statements.

A strong-willed CEO—and there are not many who are not—can often suppress the open discussion that a CFO must have with his or her audit committee.

The relationship between the chair of the audit committee and the CFO is perhaps the second most important, after that between the chairperson and CEO. And who chairs the audit committee is arguably the most critical appointment any chairperson can make. This person must have both a fundamental grasp of accounting and a backbone stiff enough that they are willing to ask all the difficult questions. Any public company board chair of audit who does not meet these two criteria should serve as a red flag for any potential investors in the company. Our board audit committee chairs at SNC-Lavalin were outstanding and well qualified experts.

The chair of audit also needs to invest time in building a one-on-one relationship with the CFO. This relationship should be nurtured so that the CFO will always be willing to let the audit chair know if something does not smell right.

In our portfolio of companies, we will replace any CFO who we have even the slightest bit of doubt about. The CFO is the left tackle for the company. A great left tackle prevents the quarterback from being sacked and a great CFO prevents the kind of troubles we had at SNC-Lavalin. We were let down on this front at SNC-Lavalin in 2011.

I also believe that there would be value in term limits for the audit firm—a fresh set of eyes every ten years would help maintain objectivity (many banks already do this). In a 1984 majority opinion of the US

Supreme Court, the chief justice articulated the importance of auditor independence: "The independent auditor assumes a public responsibility transcending any employment relationship with the client. The independent public accountant performing this special function owes ultimate allegiance to the companies' creditors and stockholders, as well as to the investing public. This public watchdog function demands that the accountant maintained total independence from the client at all times and requires complete fidelity to the public trust."

And yet this public trust has been shattered often. Virtually every major accounting firm has dropped the ball on client audits. The most famous example is the Enron/Arthur Anderson debacle. But they were not alone. Both KPMG and Deloitte were fined $50 million by the US SEC for cheating on exams. PWC over the past thirteen years has faced $450 million in fines and settlements related to flawed audits and other misconduct. One of the other major firms audited one of our portfolio companies and missed very obvious signs of fraudulent accounting by our former CFO. A fresh set of eyes would catch problems earlier. An accountant should be promoted more for being a great auditor rather than for generating more business.

Many auditors are soft on their clients because one of their best career paths is to join your client in their finance department. I believe that any individual who has audited a company should be prevented from joining that client for a period of two years. Additionally, as is now generally done, the outside auditors should not be able to work on non-audit work for their client company. No tax work and consulting. The outside audit firm should worry less about keeping the company as a client and generating additional spend and more about making sure they are doing detailed audits. Capital markets depend on auditors ensuring that financial statements are accurate.

One of the fundamental differences between my experience as a private equity owner and board member, compared with my many years as a public company director, is with respect to the amount of information and analysis that I am given to fulfill my role as a responsible director. Directors of public companies are sent board books hundreds of pages long that they are expected to digest and analyze so that they understand exactly what has happened in the business. In the private equity world, I always have analysts on my teams who can digest this sort of information and do detailed analysis. That gives me the very important questions and issues that I need to raise at the next board meeting.

I think every board should be assigned a board financial analyst who would be the liaison between the CFO and the directors. This analyst would review the relevant data in the board packages and summarize it so that the directors aren't swamped but can concentrate instead on asking the hard questions. Directors would still need to do their own work but this resource would leverage their time and skills.

I would see this as being a fantastic role for someone who came from one of the accounting firms, who would then go back to their firm after having served two years in the position. This person should not come from the current auditors of the company, and it should be seen as a privilege for the individual. But it would also be a role that would bring tremendous value to the board.

SNC-Lavalin did have an Internal Audit Department and a VP International who was meant to review and approve agent contracts such as the ones that Riadh Ben Aissa was signing. Somehow this was not done. In her book *Why We Act*, social psychologist Catherine Sanderson, a professor at Amherst College, pointed out that often it is better to have just one person responsible for monitoring rather than two. She uses the example of a study about finding faults at an automated chemical plant. When a quality supervisor worked alone only 10 percent of faults were not detected. But when they worked with a partner, some 33 percent of faults were not detected. Perhaps several people at SNC-Lavalin assumed that it was someone else's job to review agent contracts or that someone else would report the smoke.

Before the troubles, SNC-Lavalin did not have a compliance department or compliance officers. In retrospect, this was certainly a mistake. Companies in the financial sector, mining, aerospace, telecommunications, and engineering and construction, that have complicated, and very large global contracts would all do well to make sure that they have compliance departments.

SNC-Lavalin hired, as we have discussed, a senior compliance officer and he brought many of the lessons that he had learned at Siemens to SNC-Lavalin as CEO Bob Card rebuilt the company. SNC-Lavalin went from having no compliance department to spending millions of dollars each year to ensure that the Libyan affair was never repeated.

Monitoring of contracts and payments to agents should be a regular board agenda item. We did discuss agent commissions on several occasions during SNC-Lavalin board meetings, but this was done on an ad hoc basis. Given that we had a vice president who handled all agent contracts, we believed we were adequately covered with respect to oversight. In hindsight, we should have had at least two reports to the board each year showing the total amount spent on agents worldwide (by agent, country, and contract). This report should have shown dollar amounts paid and also what percentage of the contract's value this amounted to.

This may not have helped in the case of SNC-Lavalin, given the deception carried out by the CEO and his EVP and division finance head, but it is best practice. This is especially important for those companies operating in some of the less transparent countries.

I am also a strong advocate for cultural and ethical training. This is particularly important in companies that operate in as many countries of the world as SNC-Lavalin did and does. All these countries had different laws and different cultural norms, and executives working in those countries must know the exact guidelines that they must follow to remain within the bounds of the law.

Once SNC-Lavalin experienced its troubles, the company brought in an extensive training program for all employees and directors to ensure that people would know when funds could be dispersed and how to handle particularly tricky ethical situations. Such as, when might it be appropriate for an employee to pay a sum of money? One might think that there is never a time to make a "facilitation payment," but in the training we did allow an exception where a person's life is in danger.

This kind of training, especially when it deals with the gray areas of ethical behavior, is particularly helpful to employees who may not know exactly what the guidelines are. We certainly should have done more of it before we ran into issues in Libya.

6. Honest and Open Board Communication

In order to have honest and open board communication, the chairperson must make sure that they build a cohesive board. A well-functioning board can discuss difficult issues openly and its members can disagree with one another. Being able to disagree means having a foundation of trust that is built over time.

Good boards also make sure that they provide enough quality in-camera time after every board meeting. Board members should also spend time outside of the formal board meetings. By that, I mean times when the board is together but not focused exclusively on business. I have found that boards generally do not invest enough time in getting to know one another. With SNC-Lavalin, many of the directors lived in Montreal. What that meant was that after board meetings or dinners, most directors headed home, without bothering to get to know one another.

The CAE board, by contrast, consisted mostly of directors from outside Montreal. The company put them up at the Queen Elizabeth Hotel, often on the same floor, and they would invariably meet for a nightcap. This not only built rapport, but it was often when directors discussed sensitive issues that were not being adequately addressed by management in the board meetings.

The best situation I ever encountered with respect to this aspect of board interaction was the Sobeys board. The reason here was specifically geographic. Our board meetings were held in Stellarton, Nova Scotia, and the out-of-town directors all stayed in the same house provided by Sobeys. So we spent many hours getting to know one another after board meetings, chatting after dinner or over breakfast. These times were when we discussed and ironed out many of the trickiest issues.

When the board meets, it is also important that the chairperson understand that they must speak last. The only way to make sure that other directors will fully voice their concerns is to make sure that the issues have not already been resolved by the chair and CEO before the discussion has even happened.

I sat on one board where the chairman and the CEO and two other very high-profile directors basically discussed all controversial issues in some detail before we had the actual board meeting to arrive at a conclusion. This certainly does not lead to open and honest communication and disenfranchises many of the directors. This also sometimes happens in tightly held or family-controlled public company boards. The chair must ensure that all voices are heard.

When I was chair at SNC-Lavalin I also chose to not sit at the end of the long rectangular board table, but rather in the middle, on the side. This made clear that I was part of the board and not there to dominate it.

An even better arrangement for a boardroom table would be to have a circular one. This leads to better communication because everyone feels equal around it. An interesting historical anecdote: on October 9, 1789, following bread riots and a march on Versailles, King Louis XVI of France had to move the Assembly from Versailles, where folks sat around an oval table, to Paris, where it could only fit a long rectangular table. Shortly thereafter we had the French Revolution. Certainly not the main cause of the revolt, but an argument for round tables, perhaps.

I often found it useful to canvass all directors before some critical board meetings to make sure that I had their views *before* they were subjected to the groupthink of the entire board. On particular issues I found that having them vote and tell me their reasons as to why they were voting a certain way, after we had received the board book, but before the meeting led to much more detailed discussions at the actual meeting.

I used exactly that mechanism when the board was trying to decide whether or not to sell SNC-Lavalin's stake in Highway 407. Having a few devil's advocates and knowing who they are before the actual meeting helps ensure that all issues and points of view are considered, especially on critical decisions. I have also found it useful to go around the table at the end of board meetings to ask each director if they had any other issues they wanted to discuss or to raise.

7. Executive and Director Compensation

Compared to other large companies, SNC-Lavalin was not particularly different on any aspects of compensation. My suggestions regarding this have more to do with companies in general to make sure that senior leaders focus on long-term, rather than short-term, results. Charlie Munger, Warren Buffett's long-time partner at Berkshire Hathaway, famously said "when you have a dumb incentive system, you get dumb outcomes." One of my favourite Harvard Professors, Bill Sahlman, taught us that when we saw a broken system we should look at the incentives. As he constantly lectured, "incentives drive behavior."

Much is made of the fact that CEOs make 324 times more than the average worker. I do not believe that CEOs are overpaid. The best athletes, actors, and professionals in all fields make many multiples of what these same positions earned fifty years ago. LA Dodgers pitcher Shohei Ohtani will make $700 million over the next ten years. There are currently more NBA players being paid $30 million per year than there are S&P 500 CEOs guaranteed the same amount annually.

I do believe, however, that CEOs should be paid on the basis of performance. But all too often, they are paid solely on the basis of sitting in the CEO's chair. Lest one believe that a CEO does not make a difference, one need only consider the case of SNC-Lavalin where one CEO did so much harm to the company and its shareholders. Over the past few years, I have given a talk to all our portfolio company senior executives on my "rule of 3" for compensation. If you look at the best three goalies in the NHL they make a little over $10 million each year. The average goalie salary in the NHL is $3.5 million and the three lowest paid goalies make $1.2 million. So, the average goalie makes three times the bottom goalies and the best goalies make three times the average. This same relationship holds if you look at most professional sports including soccer. We should pay executives based on performance as is done in the world of sports.

It is not, and should not be, a one-way street, however. In my private equity world, executives are expected to have significant amounts of "skin in the game," so that their goals are aligned with those of the ultimate owners of the company. They also are not able to take any of those gains off the table until we as the ultimate owners have been able to sell the company we have invested in successfully.

This principle would help public companies as well. CEOs should be thinking long-term and should not be trying to time their sales of shares or options to maximize their winnings based on a short-term outlook. It is a mistake to allow senior executives to receive large amounts of options and then turn around and cash them in, They should be invested in their company. Much of the after-tax gains from their options should be reinvested in the shares of the company.

I also believe that it is important to make sure that CEOs and CFOs cannot cash in all of their options and shares immediately upon retirement. That would help to make sure there are outstanding internal candidates to replace them and that all the financial statements at the time of their departure are accurate. These executives should be required to hold a portion of their shares and options for at least one or two years after they retire.

Contracts for the senior executives should also have very strict claw back provisions so when there are any abnormalities in the financial statements, they are in the same position as the shareholders when it comes to any future losses.

Had SNC-Lavalin's CEO had more of a focus on the long-term value he was creating for himself, I suspect that he would have thought differently about the decisions he made with respect to Libya and Riadh Ben Aissa.

Similarly, directors should have significant skin in the game too. It should be at least a multiple of four times what they're being paid to be a director. All of their cash compensation should be turned into shares until they have reached that level of share ownership. This will ensure they think like the very shareholders they represent.

8. Director/Senior Executive Mentorship

I discussed earlier the importance of the relationship between the chairperson and the CEO and between the chair of the audit committee and the CFO. I think relationships between other directors and senior executives are also particularly important. It is vital that individual directors have ways of understanding what is going on in a company and at the same time have a chance to meet the executives who are leading its various divisions.

We did this on an ad hoc basis at SNC-Lavalin, but I would strongly recommend that each and every director on a board should be assigned a senior executive who he or she is expected to have dinner with and to visit at their place of business at least twice a year. This would develop a trusting relationship between them. This would help directors better understand the business. And they in turn might serve as a source of information on important topics that the director should be raising at future board meetings.

I also believe that this is an excellent mentorship opportunity for younger executives. Many directors have had senior executive experience, and they could act as coaches to these executives and pass on some of their knowledge.

9. Setting the Board Agenda

The agenda for meetings should be set by the board, led by the chairperson and not by the CEO in isolation. Agenda setting is one way that strong CEOs make sure they can talk about the things they want to talk about rather than the items that are most concerning to directors.

CEOs also sometimes make sure that there isn't enough time to talk about major issues by putting them late in the agenda when the time is squeezed. When I chair a board, I solicit input from other directors and then discuss the proposed agenda with the CEO. As mentioned earlier, it is critical to leave enough in-camera time (board directors meeting without management present). Boards that fail to consistently schedule sufficient quality in-camera sessions are violating a cardinal sin of good governance.

CEOs often dislike in-camera sessions but it's important that directors get to discuss many sensitive issues and critical decisions without the CEO present. One board I sat on had an annual dinner that included only outside directors.

I am staggered at how different the agenda is for my private equity boards compared to the public company boards that I have served on. McKinsey, in a June 2011 survey of 1,597 corporate directors found, that only ten percent of board members felt they had a solid understanding of the dynamics of the industries they operated in and only twenty-one fully understood how their business created value. This is unacceptable.

A survey of Canadian directors done by McKinsey for the Canadian Coalition for Good Governance found that directors said they spent 70 percent of their time looking at the past and present and only thirty percent looking at the future. They spent 20 percent of their time looking at strategy. When asked what amount of time they should spend they said they should spend 60 percent of their time looking at the future and 40 percent looking at strategy (i.e., double the time they were currently spending).

This is exactly the difference that I have observed between private equity boards and public company ones. Far too many public company boards spend too much time on issues that are best dealt with by management. Health and safety are very important, but I have been on boards that spent twice as much time on this issue as they did on approving a billion-dollar acquisition that had the potential to make or break the company.

Essentially this is cover-your-ass behaviour. The board wants to be able to say that they have looked at every issue from health and safety, to diversity, to child labor in the Third World in case there is ever a lawsuit filed. But this then leaves them little time for the critical matters that the board's bosses, the shareholders, care about, a focus on creating shareholder value. Basically, boards are often majoring in the minors.

I think this is the "law of triviality" at work. We spend too much time on the least important issues. The 1958 book *The Pursuit of Progress* captured the issue looking at three decisions made by a particular board. The first decision was about approving a £10-million power plant, and it was discussed and approved in two-and-a-half minutes. The second decision was about painting a bike shed which was a £350 expenditure and this took forty-five minutes. The third decision was about a £21 coffee machine and that discussion lasted seventy-five minutes. Farcical, but true for many boards.

10. Dealing with Shareholders

The chairman must also make a point of listening to shareholders. They are after all, the owners the board represents. As chairman I met each year with five of the top ten shareholders in SNC-Lavalin. I also had a monthly breakfast or lunch meeting with Michael Sabia, who at the time was the head of Caisse de dépôt et placement du Québec, SNC-Lavalin's largest shareholder.

It was important that I talked to a mix of different shareholders, including short-term focused hedge funds and longer-term shareholders such as the Caisse. Invariably these two very different types of shareholders came out on opposite sides of many key investment and business decisions that we had to make as a board. We had to understand both perspectives, but we clearly focused on long-term value creation, often to the frustration of shareholders who planned to hold their shares for three to six months and make a killing.

I believe that shares held for less than a year should receive different tax treatment to incentivize longer-term shareholders. No great company was built constantly worrying about the next quarter's results.

I am also very much against dual-class shares. In the 2000s, they accounted for fewer than one in ten initial public offerings on American exchanges. In the past five years they made up more than a quarter according to the *Economist*. If entrepreneurs want to raise public money, they should have to submit to one share, one vote. I had very early exposure to this issue at Oshawa Foods. The controlling family wanted to insert one of their own members as the CEO when the rest of the board did not. When the family member was not appointed, the family was able to override that decision. The shares held by the family represented only 2 percent of the economic interest but 100 percent of the votes. They were able to make a decision that affected every single shareholder by selling the voting control of the company to a competitor because they did not agree with the board's decision to not appoint their family member CEO. The family shareholders were actually paid a significant premium for their shares.

Advocates of dual class voting structures often say that they allow an entrepreneur to control the destiny of the company that he or she has founded. I agree that this is one of the benefits of such structures. Jeff Bezos created enormous value at Amazon by being able to never worry about early quarterly profits thanks to his controlling stake. But I do not understand why those shares should be traded at significant premiums to the other shares that were instrumental in building value in that company as well.

An expert I respect enormously, David Beatty, who writes extensively about board governance and is currently adjunct professor at the Rotman School at the University of Toronto, disagrees with me on this issue of the value of dual-class shares (some shares have one vote whereas other shares have many more votes) and strong family control of public companies. He thinks these shares give entrepreneurs control to focus on the long term, which would certainly have been the case in a company such as Rogers.

But if it really is about control for multiple voting shareholders then, at the very least, they should be prevented from also gaining a premium for their shares when they sell the company. At the very least this "premium" paid to multiple voting shareholders during a transaction should not get favorable capital gains tax treatment.

David Beatty's point of view is fair, and he often says that families or tightly controlled firms in Canada have performed significantly better than other companies. I personally think this is driven by their performance under the original founder.

No doubt Bombardier did well when Laurent Beaudoin was at the helm, as did CGI when Serge Godin grew the business. But there is no guarantee that the next generation will continue the entrepreneurial brilliance of the founder. If one looks not at the performance of family firms under their founder generation, but the performance after the exit of the founder, the picture is much different. As the *Economist* reported in February 2023, "one of the best predictors that a firm will be poorly managed is that it is family-owned and has a chief executive whose position is due to inheritance, and specifically to being the eldest male child." There are clearly numerous exceptions to this as demonstrated by Ted Turner in the US or Michael McCain and Galen Weston here in Canada.

These companies with dual-class shareholders also often seem to favor boards made-up of family members, family accountants, favorite professors and others close to the founder. They may not be the right directors to give real feedback to the founder. One need only look at Tesla's board to see that many directors are really Elon Musk's friends and family. Were they thinking of the other shareholders when they approved Elon's $56 billion pay package? Would Elon not have been motivated if the compensation package was $5 billion?

Good governance should set term limits on multiple voting shares of twenty-five years or the succession of the founder, whichever comes first.

* * *

So, the answer to the question, what did I learn from the SNC-Lavalin experience? After much reflection I can safely say: a lot.

There is a great deal about what happened at SNC-Lavalin that left me very angry and frustrated. It exposed serious problems with respect to board and management interactions, not to mention government policy and politics. I think a lot of bad things happened, carried out by both criminals and well-intentioned people who were either misguided or badly misinformed.

I've tried hard to be open and honest about my own mistakes and shortcomings. But I'm ultimately proud of what we accomplished. As I hope I've made clear in this story, the directors of SNC-Lavalin tried very hard to do the right thing to keep the company afloat and to protect the investors and employees. They did this despite being hammered daily in the Canadian press.

The good news is that thanks to their hard work and perseverance SNC-Lavalin still stands today. The company's share price is now higher than it was thirteen years ago. The SNC-Lavalin of today is very different from the SNC-Lavalin of 2011. The company has made enormous strides to make sure that the events that occurred in Libya would never occur again. SNC-Lavalin in 2021 earned the coveted Compliance Leader Verification from Ethisphere Institute, a global leader in defining standards of ethical business practices. As CEO Ian Edwards said "over nearly ten years, we evolved through honest reflection, hard work and a sustained commitment by and towards all our employees, leading to the integration of integrity best practices."

SNC-Lavalin was a great Canadian success story for over 100 years and today under its new name, AtkinsRealis, it continues to be a strong global engineering and construction powerhouse. It recently won an important contract to build Candu nuclear reactors in Romania. Canada should be cheering the relaunch of this Canadian icon. The company has scar tissue from the trauma of the past thirteen years, but arguably it has come out stronger and more resilient having survived the storm. Warren Buffett claims that it takes twenty years to build a reputation and five minutes to lose it. In the case of SNC-Lavalin, a reputation built over a century was destroyed over a couple of years by a few misguided senior executives.

Ian Edwards and his outstanding team have helped the company regain its mojo. Operating under its new name I am confident that AtkinsRealis will again become one of the best engineering and construction firms in the world.

Earlier I stated that I had witnessed first-hand three Acts in the SNC-Lavalin saga. After I stepped down as chairman the company experienced two more acts. The five acts of this turbulent story are best understood looking at the trajectory of the company's stock price over the past twenty-five years:

Act I covered the glory years under Jacques Lamarre. The company's market capitalization skyrocketed. SNC-Lavalin became a global powerhouse. Act II begins in late 2011 with the Mexican arrest and quickly moves to the early 2012 parting of the ways with Riadh Ben Aissa, Stephane Roy, and Pierre Duhaime. The stock price plummets and the company struggles to survive. Act III was the rebuilding of the company as first Ian and then I stepped in as chairman. By the end of Act III, the situation looked promising. Under new leadership the company was again winning high-profile contracts, and the stock price had returned to its previous high. As I stepped down as chair the future looked bright. Act IV brought the surprise announcement by Kathleen Roussel that the company would not be granted a DPA despite the fact that the government had passed a law with SNC-Lavalin in mind. Again, the stock price plummets and there is another change of leadership. Act V begins with a deal for the company with the Canadian government. Under Ian Edwards' leadership the company again rebuilds, and the stock price returns to record highs. The journey was long, but the efforts of the management team have helped strengthen the company under its new name, AtkinsRealis.

I hope the lessons that I learned at SNC-Lavalin—and they were often hard ones—will be valuable for other directors and executives going forward. I have no doubt there are other SNC-Lavalin's in the making. There will always be corruptible executives in the world. But with good directors, good relationships, and solid structures in place, these stories of corporate crime and greed can have much happier endings.

Some years ago, I attended a lecture by former Enron chief financial officer Andrew Fastow. He had served five years in prison for his role in the biggest accounting scandal in US history. He recounted being angry and bitter when he was first sentenced. What he had done had been approved by the CEO and auditors. His punishment seemed unfair, he thought.

He talked about turning to religion while in prison, where he was granted time each month with a Rabbi. Over time he came to a realization: he may not have broken a commandment, strictly speaking, but his behaviour was wrong. The bottom line of the Torah is to do good. I knew what we were doing was misleading to investors, he explained.

"There are people who look at the rules and find ways to structure around them. The more complex the rules, the more opportunity," Fastow once said, speaking to a business school class at the University of Colorado–Boulder. "The question I should have asked is not what is the rule, but what is the principle."

In the case of SNC-Lavalin, three individuals chose to do the wrong thing. They hid what they were doing. Billions were lost. People were badly hurt. My dad would often tell me to ask the question, "What do you do when no one is watching?" John McCain shared my dad's view of right and wrong. Jeffrey Golberg wrote in the April 2024 issue of the *Atlantic* that "John McCain once told me that he liked to think that 'in the toughest moments I'd do the right thing, but you never know until you're tested." John McCain was tested many times in his life starting with his time as a prisoner in North Vietnam. Many others fail the test. How you behave, at all times, defines you. I hope there are more people like my dad, like John McCain, like the new version Andy Fastow even, who understand that in business, as in life, these basic principles matter.

Appendix: The Value of Market Share

Higher market share is highly correlated with improved returns on investment. In fact, in the exhaustive study laid out in the PIMS (profit impact of market strategy) database of more than 2600 business units, the most important variable explaining a firm's profitability is its market share. As shown in the chart below business units with market shares under 10% earned just a little over 10% pretax return on investment. Those with between 20 and 30% market share earned more than a 20% ROI. And leaders with more than 50% market share earned on average 40% pretax ROI (or almost four times what the smaller players earned).

Bain & Company was more focused on relative market share rather than just absolute market share percentages. In industry sector after

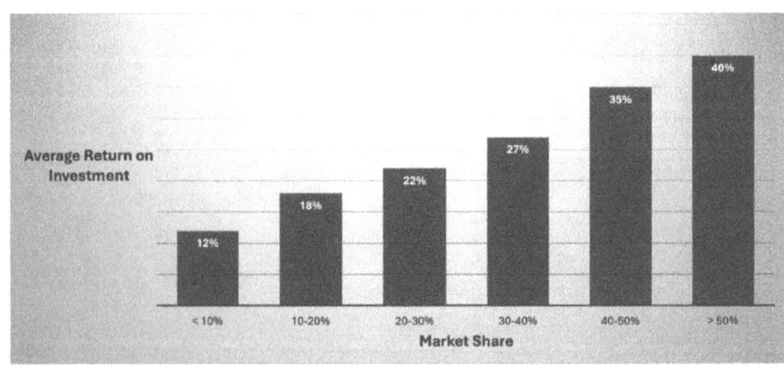

Source : PIMS 4-year average for 2611 business units

industry sector Bain found a strong and positive correlation between higher relative market share and superior ROI.

Sounds simple but the art of business strategy is business definition. What business do you compete in and what is your relative market share of this correctly defined business? Business definition must focus on two different dimensions: product/service offering and geography. In the case of SNC-Lavalin for example, we could not look at SNC-Lavalin's relative market share (RMS) based on too broad definitions of the product/service offering. RMS in the entire engineering and construction power industry was not the relevant definition. Instead, we had to look at RMS in the nuclear power industry, the gas power industry and the hydropower industry. But relative market share had to take into consideration geography. If you have the only food store in a town with the next food store some 50 miles away it does not matter that Loblaws is 100 times larger than you in the entire country. In this example, local market share counts. Similarly at SNC-Lavalin in the general engineering industry (such as building and maintaining roads) what counted was local market share. On the other hand, if you are measuring market share in the aircraft business (Airbus versus Boeing) then global market share counts. At SNC-Lavalin our market share in hydropower and nuclear engineering had to be measured on a global basis as this was the relevant market definition.

Bottom line is that correct business definition drives successful business strategies. Being able to define the specific product and service offering and geographic scope of a business is the foundation of a strategic plan. Usually, the number one or number two player in the correctly defined business sandbox will get more than their fair share of the profits. Bain's analysis of more than 4000 business units over decades has shown that more than 80% of the profit pie goes to the number one or two players in the business.

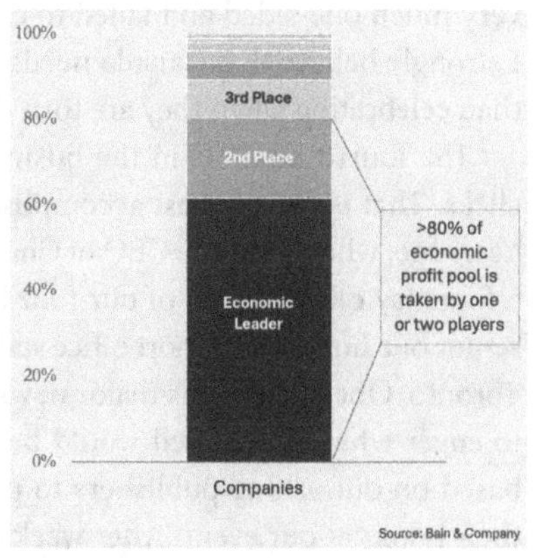

Acknowledgements

This is my story and not the official SNC-Lavalin version of the last fourteen years. The company is correctly focused on moving forward and understandably would certainly like to forget the trauma of the entire public affair. I have waited seven years from the time I stepped down as chairman as I did not want to have access to any information that was current from that time as an insider. I did not solicit input from current employees but did spend countless hours with former senior executives of the company, fellow former directors, and many former advisers to the company. This is by its nature an insider's perspective on the SNC-Lavalin story as I spent eighteen years on the board and was chairman for the last three of those eighteen years. Because of that vantage point I certainly also have a biased view. This story was covered extensively in the Canadian press, but I believed that this coverage was very much one-sided and failed to explain the company's perspective. I strongly believe that Canada needs to build global champions rather than celebrating when they are torn down.

The fourth estate is in the business of selling papers and getting clicks. That is usually best accomplished by focusing on the negative. Years ago, when I was the CEO of Chapters, I organized for the first time a four-day offsite for all of our four hundred store managers and our senior one hundred support office staff at the Deerhurst Resort north of Toronto. One of Canada's major newspapers assigned three journalists to cover what they hoped would be a negative story about Chapters based on our asking publishers to pay for speaking slots to promote their books at our event. After weeks of interviews there was no press coverage, and I asked the lead journalist why they had not written anything after all that work. She honestly answered me that it was because the publishers thought it was a great event!

Similarly, the SNC-Lavalin coverage focused only on the negative. The press felled many trees but most of the coverage was "gotcha" journalism. They were more interested in salacious coverage of yachts, champagne, and sex workers. The coverage never gave the company credit for all the changes that had been made to correct the situation. The coverage also focused extensively on the entire corporation rather than focusing on the guilty individuals. As a result, many of my business colleagues missed the true story of SNC-Lavalin. That drove me to write this book over the past four years.

I want to thank many of my former colleagues on the board who spent time with me as we tried to remember details of conversations and particular discussions from our board meetings. Their counsel was wise and much appreciated. I particularly want to thank Ian Bourne, who was the chairman before me. Ian had a ring-side seat as he was chair of the Audit Committee and then interim CEO and finally chairman of the board. Ian played a major role in helping keep the ship afloat when the troubles hit. He also had extensive notes and a great recollection of all the key meetings that we had with senior management over the very busy eighteen-month period from late 2011 through to early 2013.

I also am very indebted to Vincent Larouche's book, *La Saga SNC-Lavalin*. He did more than thirty interviews with many of the players in the SNC-Lavalin story and this helped me fill in the blanks for many parts of the story that would have been inaccessible to me. He is an outstanding journalist, and his book is a detailed and fair representation of the story. I also much appreciate that he dedicated the book to the many employees of SNC-Lavalin who had nothing to do with this saga. As he so rightly pointed out they are "the real builders."

I would also like to thank my wife Pamela and my daughter Glynnis, who both read and corrected multiple drafts over the past year. I would also like to thank my editors, Ken Whyte and Ian Coutts who both guided me to focus on key elements of the story and to discard tangents.

Finally, and most importantly I want to thank Colin Campbell. Colin helped me turn what was a chronological history of the events into a wonderful story. His extensive experience at the *Toronto Star*, *Maclean's*, and the *New York Times* made this book a much more accessible and interesting read. I enjoyed our bi-weekly meetings over the past year as he shaped the story. His business acumen and his decades of working on political issues made our discussions one of the highlights of the past year. He encouraged me to add both more depth to the events and to add more personal anecdotes to tie me more into the story I was telling.

Index